On the Home Front

On the Home Front

My Mother's Story of Everyday American Life
from Prohibition Through World War II

Mary Jo Clark
as told to Jack Clark

A PLUME BOOK

PLUME
Published by the Penguin Group
Penguin Putnam Inc., 375 Hudson Street, New York, New York 10014, U.S.A.
Penguin Books Ltd, 80 Strand, London WC2R 0RL, England
Penguin Books Australia Ltd, Ringwood, Victoria, Australia
Penguin Books Canada Ltd, 10 Alcorn Avenue, Toronto, Ontario, Canada M4V 3B2
Penguin Books (N.Z.) Ltd, 182–190 Wairau Road, Auckland 10, New Zealand

Penguin Books Ltd, Registered Offices:
Harmondsworth, Middlesex, England

First published by Plume,
a member of Penguin Putnam Inc.

First Printing, April 2002
10 9 8 7 6 5 4 3 2 1

Cover photograph: Mary Jo Clark, with son Kevin in her arms and
daughter Mary Jo at her side, 1955.
Back cover photograph: (left to right) Mary Jo Ryan, Catherine Conway Higdon, and
Marguerite Kinney Ryan at the Wisconsin Dells, before the war.

 REGISTERED TRADEMARK—MARCA REGISTRADA

"That Old Gang of Mine," words by Billy Rose and Mort Dixon, music by Ray
Henderson. © Copyright 1923 by Bourne Co. Copyright renewed. All Rights Reserved.
International Copyright Secured.

Library of Congress Cataloging-in-Publication Data
Clark, Mary Jo.
On the home front : my mother's story of everyday American life from prohibition
through World War II / Mary Jo Clark as told to Jack Clark.
p.   cm.
ISBN 0-452-28312-4
1. Clark, Mary Jo—Anecdotes. 2. United States—Social life and
customs—1918–1945. 3. Chicago (Ill.)—Biography. I. Clark, Jack. II. Title.

CT275.C6288 A3 2002
973.91—dc21   2001058846

Printed in the United States of America
Set in Sabon
Designed by Leonard Telesca

To my children
who inspired me to tell stories
and
to my mother
Maud Margaret Ethel
Cecelia Catherine Hennessy Ryan.

ACKNOWLEDGMENTS

We'd like to thank everybody at the *Chicago Reader,* especially Pat Arden, Kitry Krause, Mike Lenehan and Alison True. Also, many thanks to Tom McLaughlin, the family photo archivist, and to Gary Brozek, Steve Grossman, Sydney Lewis and Rob Preskill.

Contents

Introduction

We are all witnesses to history.

Many of us carry lost worlds in our heads—the old country, the old neighborhood. We remember friends and relatives long dead, who otherwise would be forgotten.

My mother's lost world is mostly from her childhood and young adulthood in a working-class neighborhood on the West Side of Chicago. She was born in 1914, the fourth of seven children, three of whom died young. Her father, Jack Ryan, was a marble worker, her mother, Maud Hennessy, a commercial color artist. They were both first-generation Irish Americans.

The elements of my mother's life are fairly simple—family, school, work—and fairly common. She lived through historic times—Prohibition and the Great Depression, World War II—but her experiences were not unusual. What makes her special is her ability to shape these experiences into coherent, heartfelt stories. She stops the whirlwind and we see the touch of history on the common man, and get an intimate look at everyday life in a world gone by.

Adulthood came early for my mother and for many in her generation. She left school at age fifteen, lied about her age, and went to work to help support her family.

She spent years working in the mail order business, first at Sears then at Spiegel's, while finishing high school at night. She met my father in an English literature class. They fell in love but World War II and the army got in the way. They were married while my father was on furlough from the Air Corps. My mother got a job at the ration board.

My oldest sister was born as the war was ending. My mother stayed home for the next seventeen years, raising seven children. She told us the standard childhood stories, of course—Goldilocks and the bears, the three little pigs, Noah and his ark—but she also told us stories from her past. Stories about her Aunt Nell, who'd given her children away, and Aunt Maggie, who couldn't read a word. Stories about her mother and father, her sisters and brothers. Stories about work and school, the Depression and the war.

When my youngest sister started first grade, my mother went looking for a job. She found one at Alden's, another Chicago mail order house.

One day she came down late for lunch. "Mary Jo, where have you been?" one of her coworkers asked. "We've been waiting for one of your stories." And that offhand remark eventually led my mother to the realization that she was a genuine storyteller.

After retiring in 1983, she tried to put the stories on paper but found little success with the written word. We bought her a computer for her seventy-fifth birthday. The new technology didn't help her realize her dream. She still told her stories but now with a bittersweet tinge. When she died the stories would probably die with her, and that would be the end of Aunt Nell, whom she had loved so much, of Uncle Percy, whose name was not really Percy, of Dusty Rhodes, who'd repossessed the furniture on Christmas Eve, of her old boss Henderson, who didn't believe in funerals, and of Ma and Pa, of the coloring business and the marble trade. For most of them, long gone, she was the last link to this world.

I volunteered to interview her, and then I spent some time weaving the interviews together into a 160-page manuscript, more or less in chronological order. We photocopied the pages and bound them, and my mother gave everyone in the family a copy for Christmas.

The present was a success, or so it seemed.

But there was something missing. I wasn't sure what. A few months later, I sent the manuscript to Mike Lenehan, an editor at the *Chicago Reader,* a weekly I'd been writing for on and off for years.

I have to admit, I was a bit embarrassed to submit a 160-page manuscript, especially one about my own mother. But as I told Mike, I knew there was a lot of good material in it. Maybe he could figure out some way to use it.

He called me a few weeks later. "Boy, I'm glad to get that out of my briefcase," he said, explaining that he'd been lugging the manuscript back and forth on the el. But he thought he'd found something. "It has a lot of great little stories that show how the world has changed, how the city's changed. I think if you pulled some of those out, we could use them as a series."

And that's exactly what happened. The first story ran in December 1995, and the series has been running ever since under the heading West Side Stories.

As I continued to cull stories from the manuscript and then to once again interview my mother, I realized what had happened. I'd been trying to put together my mother's life story. But that wasn't what she'd been telling me. She'd simply been telling me stories from her life.

In my zest to put it all in chronological order, I'd interrupted many of them in midstream, including some family favorites.

The stories all have beginnings, middles, and endings. Frequently, there's a punch line. Some are funny, others sad. The shortest story in the collection, about President Harding's funeral train, is barely a hundred words, the longest, about my mother's Aunt Nell Hennessy, the woman who gave her children away, is twenty-four hundred. But, like most of the stories, they are both of a world that no longer exists. Except in memory.

Among my mother's souvenirs is an old penny postcard that was sent by her Uncle Percy to her Aunt Anna. She keeps it for the poem printed on the front:

> *I know not what the days may bring*
> *Of dangers wild or joy serene*
> *But turning to the east I sing*
> *Lord, keep my memory green.*

My mother is eighty-seven as I write this. Her knees are bad. Her eyesight is failing. But she still tells a good story.

—Jack Clark

On the Home Front

Pearl Harbor

We were downtown at the library studying on Sunday afternoon, December 7, 1941. Vince went out to Washington Street to have a smoke, and he came back with the extra— PEARL HARBOR BOMBED. I remember that we picked up our books and got on the el, and I cried all the way home.

And then the next day, Monday, I went to work, and everybody was in a panic. President Roosevelt was going to speak, so the whole company stopped work to listen to him. This was the "day of infamy" speech, where we declared war on Japan. Then afterwards Modie Spiegel got up there.

He was the president of Spiegel's, and he used to come to the cafeteria to eat his lunch with everybody else. One day he got his sleeve in the soup bucket. He laughed. Everybody thought it was so funny—the president of the company with his sleeve in the soup bucket. That would never have happened at Sears. They'd be in the executive dining room.

But anyway, after Roosevelt's speech Modie Spiegel got up there and said that what the president wanted was everybody to stay at his job and do his job and not to panic—and to buy war bonds. So we started buying war bonds. You could have them taken out of your pay if you wanted. I still have two of them here I have to cash in.

The Ryan Boys

The three Ryan boys came from Tipperary, Ireland, to New Orleans. Thomas, Patrick, and Philip. I don't know the year. Philip and Patrick were both stonecutters. That's all we know about the family in Ireland.

They were down in New Orleans for a while, and then they heard about all these jobs in Illinois, helping to build the canals. So they came up the Mississippi, and on the way Thomas was shot by Indians with a bow and arrow. That's all the details I know, except that he lost an eye. He always wore a patch.

Thomas never married. He was the bachelor uncle. Cousin Nancy said he always told them stories of his adventures— coming up the river and so on—and some of them she felt were things he made up just to keep them entertained.

So they built the canals, and then Philip and Patrick married the McLaughlin sisters, Nancy and Ellen, whose family lived on a land grant around 131st and Wolf Road. It was a homestead.

Thomas McLaughlin, my great-grandfather, gave each couple forty acres. But neither of the Ryan boys being farmers, they didn't stay there very long.

My grandfather, Philip Ryan, came to Chicago with his children after his wife, Nancy, died. Nancy was mother of Tom, Ed, John, James, Margaret, Joe, Anna, and Rose. John was my father, Jack Ryan. He was born in 1873, two years after the Chicago Fire.

Philip Ryan got into the marble business in Chicago. Later his brother Patrick came to Chicago and got into the saloon business.

Philip let his farm go, but Patrick's side of the family kept their part of the land down there by having someone live on it. The farmhouse was a shack almost. They had cows—a couple of cows, which Will used to take out to graze or whatever you call it. They had chickens and stuff like that, apple and pear trees, but they didn't do any real farming.

It wasn't a beautiful farm, but it was beautiful land. It's now part of the forest preserve, the Tampier Slough.

Some of Patrick's children stayed on the farm, and some of them came to the city. Cousin Nancy took an apartment at 12th and Crawford, now Roosevelt and Pulaski. Blanche stayed on the farm.

The apartment had a big Chicago bay window. You could look down 12th Street and Crawford Avenue, and as kids, we felt like you could see the whole world going by, with all these streetcars and wagons and horses and whatever else. It was upstairs of Stamm's Drugstore. Nancy, Will, Art, and Jim lived up there. And Blanche and Leo and Phil lived out at the farm.

They kept the farm until—well, Blanche died. Nancy died out there. She moved back out there later. Will died before Nancy

*The front porch of the family farmhouse, late 1800s. That's
Philip Ryan, my grandfather, just in the picture* (far left),
great-grandfather Thomas McLaughlin (far right) *next to
his wife, Margaret, cousin Nancy, and Blanche, and some of
the Ryan boys in between.*

and Blanche. And then Jim was out there at the farm by himself. He was the only one there. This is the late '40s.

Somebody came around buying up land, and he signed the farm over for a few hundred dollars. So that was the farm.

Anyway, Jim got sick, and he went to County Hospital. I don't know if he had cancer or what. But I remember that my father went down to visit him. He stayed most of the day, and then he came home. And he was only home a short time when he got a call saying Jim had died. I said, "Pa, why didn't you stay with him?"

And he said, "I couldn't stand it any longer, watching him die."

Why did none of Patrick's children get married? Nancy, Blanche, Phil, Will, Leo, Art, and Jim—none of them ever married. We asked Nancy one time why none of the boys married, and she said whenever one of the boys brought someone home, if it looked like things were going to get serious the girls always made trouble.

So of all those kids—fifteen kids that the two Ryan boys had—my father was the only one to have children. Two of his sisters married late in life, but neither had children. And all of these others. It's amazing, the Ryans, that not one of them—Pa was the only one. He had seven, and three died young. Isn't that something?

My Mother Could See the Depression Coming

My mother could see the Depression coming for our family before the Depression actually hit, because of all the strikes and stuff that my father was on.

In 1927, when my older sister Marge was ready to go to high school, Ma said, "You've got to take a two-year commercial course so you can learn something that you can earn a living with." We found out that Providence High School had a course where you learned typing, shorthand, bookkeeping, and commercial law, all in two years. You got a commercial degree.

My mother's theory was, if you learned how to do something you could advance yourself. You could get into an office, and you won't have to be a housekeeper like these Irish girls, come over from Ireland and all they can do is clean house.

So when I was in first year they came to the room and said there was one vacancy in the algebra course. Was there anybody in the commercial course who wanted to take it? So I took it. This was part of the academic course, where you took algebra and geometry and science and all that. We just took typing, shorthand, bookkeeping, commercial law, and religion. Five subjects. No history.

I can't remember taking English as English. But when you got out of eighth grade at Our Lady of Sorrows you were supposed to know English, and we did. The sisters saw to that.

I took the algebra class and got a feeling for it, and then I wanted to go on and do more school. But instead I left school in my second year.

Someone that my mother knew from the Court Douglas Lodge heard about this job where they needed someone right away. So I left school near the first of May 1930 to take the job. Missed the graduation, the whole bit. I would have had to go to June to graduate. Since I didn't have my tuition paid, I wouldn't have got the diploma anyway. Years later I did go back and get the diploma. I paid the tuition.

So I left school and went to work at the Jay Company. It was an old building at Clinton and Jackson across the street from the Mercantile Bank. The company was owned by two men, Anthony and Joseph. That was how they got the name—J, A, and whatever. The Jay Company.

I was there about two months. I did everything in the office. I took dictation. I typed letters. I took phone calls. I wrote out orders—anything they wanted done. I could type 60 words a minute. And take dictation, 125 words a minute. I'd had a course in business law where you learned about checks and that sort of stuff—bills of sale, invoices. So I knew all that stuff, and I wasn't even sixteen years old.

But that was because my mother was very smart. She could see the writing on the wall, and she knew that we'd need to go to work to make money to keep the house going.

Well, anyway, orders weren't so good. They weren't making any money, so they asked me if I would go in the factory and wire lamps. Which is probably the only practical thing I ever learned in my whole working life. I can still wire a lamp when I need to.

So I stood at a table and wired lamps. I'd be looking out at this big clock on Union Station, and a clock never moved so slowly. I was insulted that I should be doing factory work. This is at sixteen.

I always brought my lunch, and at lunchtime I'd eat in a hurry. Then I'd walk all the way down Jackson to Michigan, and then I'd turn around and walk back. I'd never go in a store and look or anything. I just walked. It was strange. And I felt so lost in this great big world out there. I knew nobody, so it was safe to be inside wiring my lamps.

Besides lamps, they also made radio benches. They were sort of kidney shaped, with an upholstered seat. People put them in front of their radio and sat and listened. They also made bookends. "Old Ironsides."

One day I told the boss that I liked those bookends. I said, they're very nice. And he said, you can have a pair. He called the factory boy in and said, "Would you paint up a pair of bookends for . . ." They were metal ships. They painted them black. He said, "Paint up a set of these bookends for Jo to take home. In fact, if you like 'em you can take a set home too."

The kid said, "Oh, I took a set home last night." That finished him. "You're fired," the boss said.

Anyway, you don't take the boss's stuff home without asking, that's for sure.

The Sinking of the Dorchester

All of our people were drafted. Nobody joined. I don't know anybody who was a volunteer. Nobody I know. They all had a number. When their number came up, they went.

My younger sister Rosemarie, her friend Bill went in December of '41. He was Greek. His family lived on Adams Street, down near Cicero Avenue.

Ma used to say, "Why do you want to marry a Greek? His mother doesn't even speak English."

And Rosemarie would say, "You want me to marry an Irishman?"

Anyway, when Bill was shipping out for Europe, he wrote and asked Rosemarie if she would come to Providence, Rhode Island, and spend a week with him before he left.

And my mother was, "No. No. No. You don't do that sort of thing. That's . . ."

But Bill rented a room for Rosemarie and he had this woman

write a letter to Ma saying that she was renting the room to Rosemarie and that she would assure her that nothing was wrong. That they would not . . .

So Ma let her go.

Afterwards, Ma was so grateful that she had because if she hadn't . . . It would have been awful.

One night, after Rosemarie got back, I woke up in the middle of the night and I found myself sitting up in bed thinking, somebody must be in trouble. One of the few times in my life I thought I must be psychic. And then I thought, well, whoever it is, I'll just say a prayer for him and go back to sleep. Which is what I did.

And it was a very few days later, I don't think it was a week, it was a Sunday, it was Valentine's Day, and Bill's brother came walking up to the house. And I thought, oh, Bill's brother is bringing Rosemarie a Valentine. He rang the bell and handed Rosemarie the telegram.

Bill was on the *Dorchester*. It had been sunk off the coast of Greenland. That's where the four chaplains gave up their life jackets and went down with the ship. It was a troopship that was sunk by a German U-boat.

I used to keep notes on a calendar at work. I'd write little things, how the war was going and who was where. And I checked back, and the night I woke up was the night the ship went down. And so I told Rosemarie that I thought Bill was trying to get to her and he hit me instead.

She was a wreck after that. She'd read every paper looking for articles. I don't think many survived.

I got married the next month and Rosemarie was the maid of honor. We didn't even know if she'd be in the wedding but she agreed. But we were quite worried about her.

During the middle of the mass, Rosemarie whispers, "Mary, I'm sick."

I whisper, "Vince, Rosemarie's sick."

He says, "Frank, Rosemarie's sick. Take her out."

So Frank, the best man, in real altar-boy style, he walks to the center, he genuflects, he takes Rosemarie, he goes out.

Now it's time for us to go up for the blessing, so we go up and kneel down and the priest turns around and he whispers, "You'd think they were getting married instead of you."

He broke the tension. You didn't feel so awful. It wasn't as bad as you thought.

And then pretty soon, Rosemarie was back. She'd felt sort of dizzy.

She'd been having a rough time. They never found Bill. They found some of the men frozen on rafts. There were some that survived, I believe, but not too many.

She watched newspapers for months.

Highest Percentage in Arithmetic

I've always felt that I was much loved. People loved me. My mother loved me. My father loved me. And when he sat me on his knee and blew smoke in my ear I knew that he loved me.

Didn't I tell you that one? Well, today it would be considered child abuse. But when I had an earache when I was a little kid, four or five, my father would sit me on his knee, and he would smoke his cigarette. And he would blow smoke in my ears, and my earache would heal.

That's why I don't exactly believe this thing about second-hand smoke. Of course I might still get cancer, but I've been around smokers all my life.

My father always rolled his own. One day on Flournoy Street, when I was about seven, he sent me to the corner to get him a "red book." So I just told the druggist that I wanted a red book, and he gave me the magazine *Redbook,* and I brought it home.

My father said, "That isn't what I want. I want paper to make my cigarettes." So I went back. It was a little book with an orange cover. It had a rubber band around it, and inside were all these little papers that he'd put his tobacco in. The tobacco was in a red can, Velvet Tobacco. He would put tobacco in the paper and then roll it and spit on it to seal the ends.

My mother always said that she was very grateful that he had to take time out to roll his own, because otherwise he would have smoked continuously. And he did die of cancer after years of treatments—cancer of the larynx and lungs—when he was seventy-five, in 1948.

Anyway, what I wanted to tell you about was this idea of having a self-image or self-confidence. Self-esteem.

When I was in third grade at Our Lady of Sorrows, Christmastime, I won the prize for arithmetic. I received this beautiful crib that you could stand up. It was made out of cardboard, and the Holy Family was in there—the statues. They were all cardboard. You just opened it up, and there was the whole Holy Family.

My mother said, "Take it back to the sister and ask her to write on the back of it." So the sister wrote, "To Josephine Ryan, for the highest percentage in arithmetic, December 1922."

Then every Christmas I would take the crib out to put it under the Christmas tree, and I would look on the back of it and see that I had the highest percentage in arithmetic. It always gave me this great feeling that I was very smart. I knew I wasn't as smart as I thought I was. Nobody is. But I always had the feeling that I was a smart kid, and I give my mother credit for that— for having me go and get it in writing.

My first communion, 1921, Our Lady of Sorrows.

Black Velvet Hat

My father worked a half day on Saturday, and while he was at work we kids helped clean the house. My mother cooked dinner, and the dinner would be on the table at one o'clock when my father got home. Well, this Saturday he didn't come home on time. He didn't arrive until three, three-thirty in the afternoon. And when he gave my mother his pay, half of it was gone. She was furious. So she put the dinner on the table and put her coat on and left. This was 1922.

She came back hours later. She had gone down to 12th Street and bought herself the most beautiful hat. It was a big hat, black velvet with a big brim and a tan velvet flower on the side. She said she had to wear it for years because she'd spent so much on it. The reason she did it was, he spent half the pay, she could spend the other half.

She always told that story as an example of two wrongs don't make a right. She said, "I hated myself every time I put that hat on my head. But I paid so much for it I had to wear it."

First and Last Automobile

In 1926 our downstairs neighbor told us that the man he worked for had a piano to sell. The man had bought the piano for his daughter, but she'd died, and he wanted to find somebody who would really use it. So my mother and my sister Marge and I went one night. The piano was brand new. Rosewood. Beautiful. Marge and I both played it.

My mother said, "How much?"

The man said, "Fifty dollars."

My mother said, "Well, I didn't bring my money with me. I'll go home and see. I have to consult my husband."

When we got home we found that the Kincaids had come over. They knew where there was a car for fifty dollars, and my father had bought it.

Instead of going back to the man and saying, "Well, I don't have the money now, but we really would like the piano, and we can pay a little at a time" or something, nothing was said, and he sold it to someone else.

One day the man said to our neighbor, "You know, I can't understand that Mrs. Ryan. Those girls loved that piano. Why didn't she want it?"

"Oh, her husband went and used the money to buy a car."

He said, "I'd have given them the piano."

So that was our piano.

The car was one of those Fords with the round window in the back. We were very excited about it. Of course we were all scared because we thought Pa didn't know how to drive.

We made a few trips. I remember once my father wanted to take us to his old school, a little red one-room schoolhouse that was out near the old family farm. This was where he got all of his schooling, all three years.

We drove around but couldn't find the school, and the roads were narrow and dangerous.

The last place we went to was Aunt Maggie and Uncle Bill's. They lived on a truck farm in Sycamore.

When we were leaving Aunt Maggie loaded us up with all these fruits and vegetables and a bottle of homemade wine. On the way back we had an accident. We went off the road on Harrison Street, just east of Mount Carmel Cemetery, near where the town hall used to be in Hillside. In those days it was a very small town.

They were doing some repairs on the road, and there were pipes you had to go around. As my father went to go around the pipes, a bus was coming the other way and wasn't making any attempt to move over or stop. So Pa hit the pipes, and we went in the ditch.

Everybody was out on the road, waving and yelling. I'm like

dead down in the bottom of the car, and I hear my mother yelling, "Where's Jo? Where's Jo?" By the time they got back to the car I came to. I was the only one hurt. I had a cut on my leg.

But we were all covered with red stuff from the strawberries and whatever else. The wife of the mayor came down the road and took us to the town hall, and we went in the washroom and cleaned up.

I do not recall how we got home.

The next day my father went out to talk to the town police, and they said, "Well, it's very simple. You were drunk."

"No, I wasn't. I spent the whole day with my family."

They said, "You can smell the liquor all over the car."

That was the bottle of homemade wine.

Anyway, he got the car fixed, but nobody would ride with him again. We all absolutely refused.

So he drove it to work. He was working up on the North Shore, Highland Park or one of those places. Marble work.

He was coming home one night, and the car got a flat tire. A couple of kids came along, young boys, and offered to help. They fixed the flat. My father thought they were nice kids, and he asked them if they'd like to buy the car.

They said, "Sure."

He said, "How much have you got between you?"

"Twenty dollars."

"OK, it's yours."

He gave them the car for twenty dollars.

And that was the last car we had in the family. What'd he need it for if no one was going to ride with him?

Never Say Never

When Rosemarie was eighteen, some of the girls were going to this dance at a country club. This was a big thing. It was a formal, like a prom, but not a prom. And she thought of Tom McLaughlin, who we'd met when we lived next door to his cousins. She decided he'd be a good one—right age, good-looking, sociable—so she asked him.

Tom came to the house. He didn't know how to dance and Rosemarie didn't want to go to a dance with a guy who couldn't dance. She wanted to practice with him. So he came over a couple of times, and she had some other people over too. And they practiced dancing. I don't think he had dated many girls. He was nineteen.

The night of the dance, we had a lot of people in and a photographer came. Rosemarie wanted to have her picture taken in the pretty dress. And I have a picture of her and Tom standing in front of a mirror. This was February 1939.

Anyway, they went to the formal, and they had a very nice

time. They went with another couple, one of Rosemarie's friends from Sears. The other guy was driving. Tom and Rosemarie sat in the back and the other couple sat in front.

When they were coming home, they drove to Tom's house on the North Side, and Tom got out of the car, said, "Well, good night, I had a good time." And the car drives off with Rosemarie alone in the back, and she says, "I'll never go out with that stupid jerk again," or words to that effect.

When she got home she told us what had happened and she swore that she would never go out with Tom McLaughlin ever again.

Tom got drafted not long after that, and he was just about ready to get out of the army when the war started. So he was in for the duration.

When the war ended, Tom was in Europe and they finally sent him home. Nineteen forty-five; he'd been in for six years.

Well, in those years he was gone, my sister Marge used to go over to his house to visit his sister Mary Ellen and her mother. One day, after the war, she went over there for dinner and Tom was lying on the couch. And she said, "What are you doing with yourself, now that you're out of the army?" And he said, "Not much of anything." And she said, "You know, that's what my sister Rosemarie is doing." Because Rosemarie's boyfriend, Bill, had gone down on the *Dorchester*. So Marge said, "Why don't you give her a call." He did, and they started going out together.

When we came home from Florida in December of '45, it was all set. They were engaged. They were married in May of '46. But Rosemarie would never admit that Marge had anything to do with it. She said, "I used to write to him now and then when he was in the service." I said, "You wrote to him, I don't remember that."

Colton, California

My father, Jack Ryan, had worked since he was very young. He only went to third grade. Then his mother died, and he stayed home to take care of his younger sisters. Eventually he followed his father into the marble business.

Around the turn of the century he left Chicago and went to the West Coast. He spent ten years out west. He worked on the state capitols in Sacramento, California, and Boise, Idaho. He also worked on something in Spokane, Washington. He talked about hearing the coyotes at night.

While he was in California he found a short-order restaurant that was for sale alongside the railroad in Colton, and he wanted to buy it. So he wrote to his father and two sisters and asked them to come out to the West Coast and help him run it. They wrote back and told him he was out of his cotton-picking mind. He never got over that. He always used that as an example of lack of family cooperation.

In 1959 Vince and I took a trip to California. We went to Colton, and we found a little restaurant alongside the railroad tracks. It was the only place around that looked like a short-order restaurant, and we went in and had a cup of coffee and a piece of pie. Of course the town had changed a lot in all those years.

In 1909 my father came back to the Midwest to work on the state capitol in Madison, Wisconsin, and he met my mother, Maud Hennessy, on a visit to Chicago. She was a girlfriend of his sister Anna. He went back to Madison, and they corresponded.

Anyway, he married my mother in 1910, and that was the end of his traveling.

He worked on the old First National Bank building, which was torn down. Union Station. He dropped his glasses. He was on a scaffold putting the ceiling in, and his glasses fell all the way to the floor. They didn't break. He never got over that.

The last big marble job he worked in Chicago was the Stevens Hotel, now the Hilton. This went up in 1926, '27, '28, but when it was finished there was no more work to do. The marble business folded up during the Depression. The last marble job he had, he went to work in Lincoln Park in the conservatory, repairing marble work. He worked there for quite a while. What I recall about it mostly is that I worked at Sears, and one of the girls said to me, "Is your father working?"

I said, "Yes, why do you ask?" By that time people weren't asking anymore.

"I noticed you're wearing a brand-new blouse," she said.

This was when the Depression started lifting, 1933, '34—it got a little better then.

I always felt terrible, though, when I thought about what

happened to him, that when he was fifty-five there wasn't any work anymore. Except these little odd jobs he got. At age fifty, it must have been very terrible to think that he had these kids and he couldn't work.

He was never well-off. Even before the Depression there were always the strikes. He was a very loyal union guy until he was old. Every now and then my father would ask my mother how much money we had in the bank. She'd tell him, and he'd say, "I thought we had more than that."

She'd say, "Well, what do you think we lived on the last time you were on strike?"

He always talked about the unions. He and Marge would argue about them at dinner. Ma would call it the dessert. "I didn't know we were going to have the dessert so early," she'd say.

In his old age my father said he wished he'd been a fireman, because then he'd have a pension.

Pa made about forty dollars a week as a marble worker. If he worked overtime, maybe fifty or sixty dollars.

During the Depression what he finally got was a job at the railroad as a watchman—nineteen dollars a week. He would walk around this railroad yard somewhere on the Southeast Side, and he had to pull these boxes at certain times. He had to get up from the spot where he started, and then he would walk around, pull his boxes, and then go back and sit down until it was time to do it again. My poor mother was so afraid that he would fall asleep and lose the job that she'd set her alarm clock—or sometimes she'd sit up all night—and call to make sure he was up.

Pa (Jack Ryan) on the West Coast, about 1900. He's the good-looking one with the big beer.

The Coloring Business

When the Stevens Hotel opened in 1928, it was the largest hotel in the world.

But when the job was done there was no more work to do. The Loop was built, my father said. "There's no space for anything else." He ought to come back and look at it.

So he went to Detroit to work. There was some marble work there. Some job that lasted about three months.

While he was gone, my mother decided that she should go back to work, because my father would never let her work. So she took all of us kids, and we went to visit her friend Josephine, who was still in the coloring business. My mother said, "Josephine, do you think I could color again?"

Josephine said, "Oh, no, Maud. You've been out of it too long. There's no chance that you could ever color again."

Oh, we were all so mad. Ma knew she could color. This was her chance. She was going to ask this woman because maybe she'd have colors and brushes she could practice with. But she gave her a flat no. "Oh, you've been out of the business too long."

The very next day we were all dressed up again, and we went downtown to the Copelin Studio on Dearborn Street to see Miss Eisart, who had been Ma's forelady. Ma said, "I've come to ask if you think I could color again."

She said, "Well, of course you could, Maud. Once you know how to do it, it's an art that you'll never forget." She said, "Here's some brushes, here's some paints, here's some pictures. Go home and practice."

So my mother went home and practiced. The next week she saw an ad in the *Tribune* for a sample color artist. You colored from the furniture or the lamp or whatnot. She answered the ad and she got the job, for a company that was having a show at the Furniture Mart on Lake Shore Drive.

Now, my mother had not worked in twenty years. But she takes herself off to the Furniture Mart and she sat there coloring. This woman who's working at the next table says, "Don't you use any alcohol?"

Ma says, "No, I don't."

"Well, what do you do when you run over?"

It was either ammonia or alcohol, one or the other.

Ma says, "I don't run over."

She came home that night, got herself out some alcohol, tried it, saw what it did. And she got ammonia, and she found out what that did.

One day this man from the Rembrandt Lamp Company saw her working in the showroom at the Furniture Mart, and he hired her to do all his pictures for his salesmen.

When my father came home from Detroit my mother was sitting at the little black table that's now in my dining room with stacks of photographs. They were black-and-white photographs, and she'd paint them so the salesmen would have a natural-looking photograph. This was before color photography.

She saved our lives during the Depression by her coloring. And my father became her transportation. He would take the pictures down; he became her messenger. He would go down to pick up the black-and-white pictures and take the finished stuff back.

She would make like seventy-five dollars some weeks. Well, my father, when he had his marble job, he didn't make that much.

One summer she had so many pictures to color that she had Rosemarie and her girlfriends help out. She would set them up at card tables. She had three or four card tables between the dining room and living room. She would give them a picture and a little dish of color that she had mixed, and she would ask them to put a gold stick on a lamp or paint a rose on a lamp shade. Lamp shades were real fancy in those days. They had beads and flowers. She just had these girls do one little thing, and they did fine. A simple thing.

But these kids, they were like eleven, twelve. She paid them a dollar a day. They loved it.

Not too long ago, at Tom McLaughlin's wake, Kathleen Kane, who's now Kathleen Walsh, came up to me. I hadn't seen her in years. She said, "Do you know that your mother was my first boss?"

I said, "Oh, the coloring business."

She said yes. And she said, "That first five dollars that your mother gave me for my first week's work, I ran home with it, across the street, and my mother ran to the Edison company and had the lights turned on. That was the most wonderful money I ever made."

Ma (Maud Hennessy), about 1895.

Eddie's First Dog

Let me tell you how my brother Eddie got his first dog. It's one of the stories I tell my grandchildren.

One Saturday while we were living on Polk Street in 1925 or so, my mother called Ed, who was about ten, and said, "Eddie, get your little wagon and go to the bakery shop. And Jo, you'd better go with him."

Ed had a little red wagon with a handle on it. So he and I went to the store at the Ward's bakery factory down near Washtenaw Avenue. What we were buying was five dozen hard rolls at a penny apiece. So we got sixty rolls for sixty cents, and that would do us for the weekend. We came out with two paper bags filled with these rolls. Maybe I was eleven and he was eight.

Anyways, what appears is a little brown dog. We decided that he looked very hungry, so we gave him a piece of a roll. And then we gave him another piece. Then we walked another block, and he was right behind us, so we gave him some more. When we got home we took the rolls in and put them on the table, and my mother said, "Thank you. That was a great job." Then she looked out in the backyard and she said, "Where'd that dog come from?"

We said, "He followed us from the bakery."

She said, "Ed, that's a very nice dog, and he belongs to somebody. Now you take him right back to where you found him and leave him there."

So Ed went back with the dog, but the dog wouldn't leave Ed. The dog came back with him. Ed said, "He keeps chasing me. I can't . . ." So it got late that night, and it was kind of cold out. So Ma said, "Well, bring the dog in. He must be starved." She put a little rug at the door, and she said, "He can sleep there, and I'll give him something to eat."

In the morning she put him out and opened the gate and said, "Now go where you belong."

Well, he ran around the yard all day while we were at school, and when we came home he was still there.

That night, Ma's feeling sorry for the dog again, so she calls him in and she feeds him. So after doing this three or four nights, well, you know, the dog's never going to go.

So she got very desperate. After we went to school the next day she took the dog and she got on the Harrison streetcar and stood on the platform in back. The conductor said it was OK as long as the dog didn't bite anyone.

So Ma went to visit a friend who lived near the bakery. She left the dog on the street and told him to go find himself another spot, " 'Cause I'm through."

So she and her friend had a nice afternoon, and when she got downstairs there was no sign of the dog at all. So she left and rode the streetcar down to Sacramento and walked home. She walked into the kitchen and put the kettle on.

She looked out the window, and what do you think she saw in the backyard? The little brown dog.

Anyway, the landlady came downstairs, and my mother explained what had happened.

"Well, don't the children like the dog?"

"The children love the dog."

"Then why do you want to get rid of it?"

"Well, because I didn't think you wanted a dog in the building."

"It's perfectly all right with me," the landlady said.

And that's how Ed got his first dog, Brownie.

We had Brownie for quite a long time, and then on the day that Margaret Fitzgerald, age seven, was buried, the dog disappeared.

Rosemarie was a pallbearer, and Ma wanted to go to the funeral mass. So she let Brownie out the back door, and she said, "I won't be here when you come back, but you can wait for me." She told us, "He kind of smiled at me, and off he went."

And we never saw him again. That's how she told it—"He kind of smiled at me."

We said, "You know, Ma, dogs don't smile."

She said, "This one did. He knew where he was going."

Margaret Fitzgerald—they lived in back of us. She had heart trouble. The pallbearers were all her little friends, dressed in their First Communion dresses.

President Harding's Train

⌘

Did I tell you about when President Harding died? I was nine. August 1923. We lived on Flournoy Street. And the train with his body was going by on the freight line that ran north-south about Washtenaw Avenue.

Anyways, we were all going down to see it pass. But my father said, "I'll go down first to see what's going on." He came back and said, "The crowds are terrible. We'll just stay here in the yard and we'll be able to hear the train whistle." So we stayed in our yard and heard the whistle as the train went by.

Aunt Nell Havern

My Aunt Nell Havern was a very, very happy, outgoing woman. After her husband died, she lived with her daughter, Eleanor, and her husband, Heggie. Then she had another daughter, Marguerite, and another daughter, Lillian.

Well, Lillian would drive the car and pick up the others and they would go all kinds of places together. In the summer they would drive up to Lake Geneva or Delavan, just for the day and back. Other times they'd go downtown to a show. And sometimes they would go to Our Lady of Sorrows for one of the gangster funerals. They knew it would be a great big deal.

All the gangsters would be there, flowers galore and all the rest. They liked to see the show. And afterwards they'd ring our doorbell and we'd have visitors for the day. They'd say, Oh, we were just over at Our Lady of Sorrows for O'Bannion or O'Kelly or for some Italian guy who was just buried. There were a lot of gangster funerals at our church. I don't know if it was that other churches wouldn't accept them, but they certainly didn't live in our neighborhood. These were the big guys. And there would be all these cars with flowers in 'em. They don't do that sort of stuff anymore.

Anyway, this was their daytime entertainment. Heggie was working. The husbands didn't have anything to do with it.

Now, some time after her husband died, Aunt Nell met Mr. Lynch. He took her out a few times and he told her he wanted to marry her and take her to Europe on a honeymoon but she refused.

Then she went with Mr. Alexander. We all loved Mr. Alexander. He was a Mason. But she told him she couldn't marry him so after a few years that broke up.

Then she ran into Mr. Lynch again. He'd already married and taken somebody else to Europe but now he was a widower. So she started going with him again and she decided to marry him.

And Heggie really didn't want her to get married. He said, "Ma, if the reason you're marrying is to get a home of your own, this is your home until your dying day. It's our home but it's your home too." They were living about 4200 Jackson Boulevard, in a white stone apartment. It was a big place.

So she was married at St. Viator's. She wore a tan lace dress and a tan hat, lace; she looked very beautiful. And she was a really beautiful, well put together lady for sixty-five.

Her granddaughter was the attendant. They were going down the aisle and I was standing next to her daughter Lillian and she says to me, "There goes one damn fool."

And it did turn out that way. Looking at the life she got for herself, she really was a fool.

Mr. Lynch was older than she was. He was retired and in many ways was disabled. Even before he got sick he didn't want her to go out. She should stay home with him all the time. And so it broke up this nice outgoing life she had with her daughters.

Coats Alike

We didn't go to Maxwell Street. We'd go to Halsted between Roosevelt and 14th Street. My mother was a little afraid of Maxwell Street. It had all these open stalls and lots of people and carts going up and down. We could find everything we wanted around the corner on Halsted.

One day I went with my mother and Marge and our neighbor Mrs. McLaughlin. We were looking for two winter coats, for Marge and me. Our winter coats were always alike. We were thirteen months apart in age, and we always thought my mother dressed us as twins. But I think it was more a matter of getting the same quality for both of us. She wanted us well dressed. And if she found a bargain for one, she'd see if she could get the same bargain for the other.

On the streetcar Marge said to me, "I don't want to get a coat like yours. I don't think we should have coats alike anymore." I was probably around twenty-one. Marge was twenty-two. So we agreed we'd get different coats. We went through the racks, and I found a beautiful brown coat. It had a little fur collar and wooden buttons all the way down the front. It was a long coat, midcalf. Beautiful satin lining and well padded. I think the material was bouclé. It's a French word. It was a beautiful, beautiful coat.

And then Marge was looking for a coat. She said, "Do you mind if I get a coat like yours?" I said, "You're the one who wanted different coats." She said, "But I found one just like yours, and it fits me." She brought the coat over. These were beautiful, beautiful coats. The only difference was hers had square buttons.

So we agreed that it was OK that we had coats alike. Then my mother started on the salesman. And from thirty-five dollars each, which would have been seventy dollars, they kept arguing back and forth—and before you know it she got him down to thirty-five dollars for both.

Mrs. McLaughlin said to her, "Mrs. Ryan, don't rob the man." So she stopped there. And we came out with these two gorgeous coats, for thirty-five dollars.

Kausal Coal Company

When the Depression hit in 1929 my mother called the Kausal Coal Company one day and asked them to send a ton of coal, which was seven dollars. She'd bought from them for twenty years.

They said, "Is it cash or charge?"

My mother said, "Charge."

The man asked her to hold on, and then he came back and said, "We're sorry, Mrs. Ryan. You've always paid cash. There must be something terribly wrong that you're asking for credit."

That afternoon she got dressed up and went down to the 12th Street Store. She bought us a brand-new living-room set, including a new rug and lamps. Five dollars down and five dollars a month. She said, "Nobody will ever tell me again that I have no credit."

We were the most stunned kids in the world. By that time we were teenage, and to get a new rug and living-room set, lamps . . .

And that's how it came—because the Kausal Coal Company wouldn't give her the coal on credit.

She never bought from them again. She called another company to get her coal.

The coal was always in the shed, and you brought it up in buckets, carried it up the stairs. My dad brought it up, but when Ed got big enough that was his job, to haul up the coal.

We had a great big coal stove in our living room. What did they call it? A hot-blast stove. It burned hard coal.

Pa's Doghouse

The people who lived downstairs knew we were going to get a new piano and they wanted our old one. So our cousins were always willing to give a hand and they came out to help move it to the basement, for this little girl down there.

But they got the piano stuck in the wall when they went to make the turn and they couldn't get it out. They had to call the movers to come and get the piano out and take it down to the basement. There was this big hole in the wall.

Well, the girl in the basement, she didn't have the piano very long when her father decided that he didn't want her to have it. He didn't like the noise so he gave it back to us.

In the meantime, we had moved down the street to this nice house, a cottage really. So we took the piano back and then sometime later we got a new piano.

My father tried to sell the old piano but nobody would buy it. So he took it down to the basement and took all the metal out and hauled that out to the alley for the garbage collector. Then he took the wood and he made a beautiful doghouse out of it. It was a real old piano, dark wood with scrollwork with cloth behind it. My father took the cloth out and made a nice window for the dog. It looked out the back of the doghouse. And he took it out in the yard and put it under the tree for Brownie.

It was beautiful.

But the dog wouldn't go inside. Brownie refused to use it. And my father got so mad one day that he chopped it up and used it for firewood.

Paris Garter

When I was fifteen years old my Aunt Anna said that I could come down to the book bindery where she was a forelady and she'd give me a job at fifteen dollars a week. So I went down there, and there was my aunt running the whole show in the bindery. She would sit up on a big high platform, and she'd be doing numbering of pages. She'd be clicking her foot as she numbered these pages—she pushed the pedal that made the numbers on the pages of the book.

They were doing a book for the Red Cross on swimming, swimming instructions. It had all these small pages, and I walked around a big table and collected the pages one at a time. What do they call it now? Collating. Well, I walked around this big table and did that all day, putting these books together..

After about two weeks the job petered out, and she didn't need me anymore. So then Mrs. Derrick, Loretta's mother, worked for Paris Garter—something like that—and she said, "Well, I can get you a job there."

So I went to Paris Garter, and I was supposed to braid belts. It was piecework. But I was so slow at it that I couldn't make any money. So they decided that instead of my doing that, I would put four pieces of leather together—two white and two black—and tie them with rubber bands, so that when the girls got them they would put them in a clamp and they would braid them. So I was paid fifteen dollars a week for putting the rubber band around—fifteen dollars a week. That was like basic pay.

This was a big factory with everybody at benches. They were telling dirty jokes all the time. I didn't know what it meant, but at least I knew it wasn't the kind of talk I was used to. So I was kind of uncomfortable there, and every night I'd come home and tell my father I didn't really like being there.

One night I went home, and Pa said he had a job for me at Sears Roebuck. I'd put in an application. They had called, and he'd answered the phone. So the way he looked at it, he'd gotten me the job.

I was never so happy to go anywhere, to get away from that job.

My father said, "Twelve dollars a week. You can start Monday."

I said, "Twelve dollars? I make fifteen." My mother said, "But you don't have to spend the carfare." The streetcar was seven cents each way. "And besides that, we'll get the twenty percent discount at Sears."

The day I started, the discount went down to ten percent.

Bootleg Liquor

During Prohibition it seemed like everybody in town made their own, and one day Pa decided if everybody else could make hooch, he could make it too. So he went out and he bought himself a still, which was a great big ceramic crock. He bought malt and hops and whatever else goes into it. And he was very happy that he had this stuff fermenting in the basement. Then one day it all blew up. The still was in pieces all over the basement.

Well, Ma was the happiest person in the world. She did not want her husband making this stuff. She'd rather he went out and got it from some of these other people. She'd rather he didn't drink it at all.

Pa knew where to get it. There were many bootleggers around the neighborhood. He went different places.

One day a neighbor woman came running into our house and said, "Mrs. Ryan, I don't know what I'm going to do. I have

Patrick's still in my basement. They're expecting a raid over there."

So they had moved Patrick's still across the street to her basement and she was panic stricken. She said, "What am I going to do? My husband's a policeman."

Ma just said, "I'm glad I don't have those worries."

And then later, the son of the bootlegger married the daughter of the policeman and one of her sisters said, "I never thought the outlaws would become our in-laws."

Now, the people next door made it. But I don't think my father ever bought from them.

We had Joe, who was Italian. He made wine. And he would come in with a bottle to give my father. And my mother would say, "Joe, he doesn't need that."

And he'd say, "Mrs. Ryan, the Lord made wine. He wanted us to drink it."

The people next door, their house was on the back by the alley. So the customers would walk down this long gangway alongside our house. They'd go in the front door and then go out the back into the alley.

One day I was on my way home for lunch and there was one of their cousins passed out in a snowdrift. So I pulled him out of the snow and said, "Come on, you know where you're going." I was sure he was going to freeze to death.

I practically carried him down the street, and then in front of our house he fell in another pile of snow and I said, "Get up. You know where it is." And he got up and he went in.

Liberty Savings

We were living on Arthington Street when the Depression came. My mother would go to the bank and get money to pay the rent. The bank was on the corner of Kedzie and 12th Street. Liberty Savings. My parents always bragged about the fact that they didn't lose a penny during the collapse. They only wished they'd had more money in the bank. The bank held. It never failed.

When she got down to two hundred dollars Ma wouldn't take any more out, because she knew she might need it for an emergency.

Rent was forty-four dollars a month. But then we couldn't pay it, and it started stacking up. We paid what we could, but pretty soon we owed about eighty dollars. So they asked the landlord to come over. It was an old lady who owned the house, Mrs. Peterson, and her son. They lived out in Riverside.

The son came over one night. My parents told him that they

would try to pay the back rent but that we were going to have to move because we couldn't afford the rent anymore.

He said, "Well, my mother would want you to stay, no matter what. So I'll reduce the rent to twenty dollars a month. And if you can pay the back rent, fine. If you can't, that's OK too."

So he took the twenty dollars. And we stayed there until 1937. I remember that my father tuck-pointed the house while he was out of work. We could have bought the place later for twenty-five hundred dollars, but nobody had any money for a down payment.

Cousin Nora

Ma's first cousin Nora got married on Christmas Day. She was a Catholic, but she married Jim, who was not. My mother was horrified. It was bad enough that she got married in a Protestant church, but on Christmas Day—how could you do that?

My mother lamented that forever, but it didn't break their friendship. When Nora's first child was born, my mother was the godmother. Nora went on and had six children, and she insisted that they all be baptized in the Catholic Church. In those days they didn't ask a lot of questions, like they do now.

When Nora got sick my mother went out to see her, and they talked about seeing a priest. Nora wanted to go to confession, get her marriage straightened out, and have a priest come when she was sick. So my mother called up the parish—I think it was Help of Christians—and a priest came over. Nora told him she had been married outside the church. That was her big worry. The priest said, "I could marry you right here in this room."

Nora said, "Well, I'll talk to my husband."

Now, Nora had all these cousins that were coming to help her. She was completely bedridden. My mother was one of several who came every day. Cousin Mary came too. She brought clean sheets and pillowcases.

Anyway, Nora talked to her husband about getting married in the Catholic Church, and Jim said no. He couldn't do that. He couldn't say that he wasn't married to her before. He couldn't say that their six children weren't legitimate.

My mother had always been very friendly with the children, who were grown by now—they were teenagers or older. But now they seemed to resent her very much, and she decided that she was causing trouble for them. One of the sons said, "I wish you'd quit talking about priests and religion to my mother."

So then, for maybe a week, Ma didn't go at all. And then she gets a call that Nora has died. She was really upset. She should have been there. She could have done something.

Ma told us all before we went to the wake, "If there is no kneeler there, we will all kneel down on the floor." There was a kneeler, but there was no priest. When she died they hadn't called a priest.

So the next time the cousins got together—they always talked over all the family business, who did what and who said what and all that—Ma said, "What I cannot understand, Jim was always so good to Nora. He would give her anything she wanted. Why wouldn't he give her the only thing that was important to her?"

Cousin Mary spoke up. She said, "I told him not to. I said, 'Jim, why should you marry as if you had never been married when you have all these children?' "

Ma said, "Mary, it would have been much better if you had stayed at home with your clean sheets."

Moving to Our Lady of Sorrows

The people who owned the building where we lived wanted our flat for their son. Now, apartments were very difficult to find in 1920. So my mother and father went looking. They looked at this flat on Flournoy Street, but the man said, "No, I don't want children."

So they went to other places, and one woman said, "You have four children? Oh, we can only take three."

And my father said, "Oh, that's fine. We'll drown the youngest."

They went quite a few months without finding an apartment.

After a while the landlord, Mrs. Graham, who had been my mother's good friend, decided to evict us. She got an eviction notice against us. My father was working, so he couldn't go. My mother went to court alone and stood in front of the judge and said, "We've tried and tried, but we haven't been able to find an apartment."

Mrs. Graham said, "But judge, they never pay the rent."

My mother opened her purse and gave him all the rent receipts. She always insisted after that, "Always get a receipt for your money, 'cause you never know when your friends will turn on you." She gave the judge the receipts, and the judge said, "Mrs. Ryan, you can have as long as it takes to find an apartment."

She liked the Our Lady of Sorrows neighborhood because of the church, which was not too old at that time. So she went back to that neighborhood, and wherever she saw a sign, she'd go in. And it would be the same story, where they didn't want kids.

She went by the same house she'd gone to before on Flournoy Street and saw that there were still no curtains on the first-floor windows. So she rang the doorbell, and Mrs. Boyle came to the door. My mother said, "Do you remember, I was here before?"

Mrs. Boyle said, "Yes, I remember you."

My mother said, "Well, I was wondering if you knew where there was another apartment?"

She said, "Well, why don't you look at this apartment?"

Ma said, "He wouldn't rent it to me 'cause I have children."

Mrs. Boyle said, "He has nothing to do with it now. I own the building."

So the day we were moving, my mother was to take the children to the new house while my father stayed with the movers and to make sure the house was cleaned and everything.

My father told my mother, "Now, the easiest way to go is to get on the 12th Street car and go to Sacramento, and then you're only a few blocks away."

So here's my mother, who was a very little woman, with these three kids and with Rosemarie—who weighed twenty pounds on the day before her first birthday—carrying this child all the way from 12th Street to Flournoy, which was a block before Harrison Street. I can still remember her with these straggling kids.

We got to Flournoy Street, and my mother is just exhausted beyond belief—and she sees a streetcar going past on Harrison Street. She cursed my father. He knew there was a car on Harrison, but he thought it would be harder for her to transfer than to walk a few blocks.

So we made it. And when we got there, Mrs. Keane, who lived on the third floor, came down and brought us a big box of fruit. She said it was from Mrs. Boyle, who was out, to welcome us to our new home.

My mother loved Our Lady of Sorrows. And after she found the apartment she said, "We're never going to move out of this parish till you kids are out of school." And that's what happened. We stayed in the neighborhood until 1937.

They Never Talked About the War

One day in 1937, after we were all working or in high school, Ma's friend Mrs. Powers went for a ride on the Jackson Boulevard bus. It was a Sunday, and it was pouring rain. She saw a For Rent sign, and she got off the bus and went to a phone and called Ma. She said, "There's a big house for rent on Jackson. Don't worry about the rain. There's a sign on the house. Go get on that bus and get out there now."

So we moved from 3024 Arthington Street to 5342 Jackson, out in Austin. That was the biggest deal. God, I was thrilled to death. Austin was beautiful. You would get off the Madison streetcar at Lockwood and you would see this beautiful, clean street. I mean, shiny windows on all the stores. And the air smelled different, because there was so much green stuff growing out there. Trees and flowers—and the buildings weren't so close together. We loved it there. Austin was the best part of the West Side.

From Jackson we moved to 101 S. Menard, the first floor of a two-flat. We all loved it. Madison Street was at one end of the block and Columbus Park at the other.

Madison Street was just a beautiful street. Beautiful shops. I remember you could see the State Theater from our front porch. There was a little delicatessen where they made doughnuts. Vince would walk me home from Austin High School, and we'd stop in there and buy a few. Then we'd go over to Columbus Park and sit on a bench and eat 'em. They were delicious. I haven't had doughnuts that good since.

We used to spend a lot of time in Columbus Park. You could rent a rowboat for twenty-five cents and go rowing for an hour. We could play tennis. My mother gave me two tennis rackets and a net for my birthday. So we would do that.

There was ice-skating on the lagoon. We had a lot of good times at 101. We did a lot of things from there. We'd rent a bike for a quarter an hour—two hours for fifty cents—from this shop on Madison Street. Then we'd ride into Oak Park and River Forest and look at all the fancy houses.

But then in 1940 the people we rented from said they wanted the apartment back. So of course we were all desperate. We hated the thought of giving up Austin. So we went out walking—blocks and blocks and blocks—and the only place we could find in the neighborhood only had two bedrooms.

The apartment on Menard had three. Ed had one, Ma and Pa had one, and the three girls had the other. We had a studio couch and a full bed in our room.

Then Rosemarie and I got together and decided, if we can't find a place to live out in Austin, which we loved, then let's go back to the neighborhood near Sears, so we can at least have the advantage of walking to work.

So we went down to the Sears neighborhood and walked around, and we found this two-story, white stone building on Flournoy Street, 3608 Flournoy. It was a second-floor apartment, and it had a vacant lot next to it which was like part of the house. So we figured, well, at least you'd get a little air and sun. Of course we didn't realize about the train running in back of the house.

It was such a big apartment that it went all the way back to the alley. The biggest bedroom, which Rosemarie and I shared, had a diagonal window that looked right out on the elevated tracks. Well, the el wasn't so bad, but when that Aurora-Elgin train went by—the "Roarin' Elgin," with these big flashing lights—even with the shades down you still got all the noise and the lights. I would jump out of bed in the middle of the night and find myself standing there in the middle of the floor, and I wouldn't know where I was.

Vince would say, "Well, if you have a light alongside your bed, just flip the light on, and then you'll know that it was just a train going by."

Anyway, we moved in there around the first of September, and Marge and Bud were married on the twenty-first. While they were getting married, German bombs were destroying London and we were all hoping we'd stay out of the war.

"I hate war," President Roosevelt said. "We're never getting in the war. I hate war." That's what he said.

So Marge and Bud got married. They used to call themselves Mud and Barge. Anyway, they got married, and when we went to their house there was no music. It just didn't seem right. They were the best piano players we knew. So I came home, good-hearted, you know, and I said to my mother, "I think we should give the piano to Marge, because after all, Loretta gave it to her in the first place."

So Marge and Bud got the piano.

Bud fingered the piano so beautifully. And then when he went to the war he got frozen fingers and frozen feet. When he came back he had this Raynaud's disease. All his fingers were infected, and he couldn't play piano for a long time.

You know, a lot of them never talked about the war. Ed never talked about what he did in the war. I know he was in Europe. He might have been in the D-Day invasion. He was in Europe right after the invasion, but I never really knew. He never talked about it.

Marge's wedding, September 21, 1940, Our Lady of Sorrows. Rosemarie (left of bride), *Rosemary McIntyre* (right), *and Ma and Pa, in the background.*

They Didn't Have Married Women at Sears

In 1930, when I first worked at Sears, one of my friends got married on a Saturday—Nancy. She lived in Oak Park. She was eighteen years old.

She didn't have a big wedding or anything like that, and she came in on Monday to go to work. They called her into the main office and told her they were sorry, but they didn't have married women at Sears, so she would have to leave.

We had about two hundred people in the collection department, all on one floor. And to think there were all those women and none of them were married. But when I think back, I know I never heard of their husbands. A lot of them were older. They just had all that Sears stock they held on to—profit sharing.

I don't know what happened to Nancy. She left, and I never saw her again.

Single women from the collection department at Sears.
Mary Jo Ryan is second row, right.

The Door-Tender's Seat

When I was in sixth grade, the reward for winning the spelling bee was that you could have whatever seat you wanted. And the most envied seat was the last seat in the first row, because that was the door-tender's seat.

Another nun would send a kid with a message, and he'd open the door and hand you a note or whisper the message to you, and you'd go up and tell the sister. So you knew everything before everybody else.

Now, you could lose the seat several ways. If you were late, or if you got a bad mark on something, or if you didn't do your homework. But the person who got the seat was usually a person who did all that stuff, you know, someone who knew the score.

So, anyway, I would have the seat, and then maybe I'd be caught talking or I'd be late for school. And the sister would say, "You—get a seat over in the last row." So I'd clear out the door-tender's desk and go sit in the last row. And then about ten o'clock there'd be maybe a spelling bee, and I was a good speller. So often I won the spelling bee. And the prize was, what seat do you want? The last seat in the first row. So I would take my books and move back in. I spent a lot of time carrying my books back and forth across the room.

There was also the stand-up percentage contest, with the seat as the prize. The whole class would stand up and when your turn came if you missed the answer you sat down. Pretty soon there'd only be a couple of people standing and I was usually one of them. I was smart when I was young. What happened to me?

Libertyville Farm

In 1939 the war was going on in Europe. London was being bombarded and they were trying to get the children out. So our club, the Women's Novena Auxiliary at Our Lady of Sorrows, was looking for volunteers to go to Libertyville to help these nuns who had volunteered to take care of some children from England.

They decided to have a picnic day for the whole club and anybody who could stay for a week should come prepared to stay. So my friend Catherine and I asked for a week's vacation from Sears.

When we got there we found that the English children had not come, but we could stay anyway and work on the farm. So we decided to stay. Everybody went home toward evening. We were the only two staying, out of about forty.

A group of nuns from the Netherlands ran the place. It had been a boy scout camp at one time. They said we would stay in the old farmhouse. So we walked down the road with this girl. She must have been a nun. It was a block or more from the main settlement. There was nobody in the house. The main floor had no furniture. We went upstairs and the rooms had two cots in each. This was where the visitors would stay. Well, anyway, it looked a little spooky.

So this nun said, "Let's kneel down and say some prayers." And she started praying. I don't know why but Catherine and I started laughing and we couldn't stop. And she was horrified. "You don't act like that when you pray." Well, the more she said it the more we laughed. We just couldn't stop ourselves. So finally she said, "Well, I'll just leave you here."

In the middle of the night I woke up and I saw a light coming through the window. So I reached over to Catherine and shook her and said, "Catherine, I think somebody's out there with a flashlight." She opened her eyes and looked around and said, "That's the moon, you idiot."

The next morning after mass and breakfast we went to work on the farm. There were other people working too, people who stayed there all the time.

Anyway, we picked beans. And the sun was hot. And it wasn't easy. And then we dug in the ground for . . . Anyway, it was hard work. At noon we had lunch and then we went out to do some hoeing. So we did this for about three days, that was the routine.

It was very nice, though. At dinner there were big discussions around the table. But anyway, by Thursday we couldn't stand it any longer and we called Catherine's brother and asked if he could come out and pick us up. He said he couldn't come then, but he'd come Friday. So we went home Friday.

We were the heroes of the club, that we did it. But the English children never came. And as Catherine says, I've never taken a potato for granted since, or a bean either.

Parade of the Wooden Soldiers

When we lived on Sacramento Boulevard my mother wanted Marge and me to take piano lessons. She saw a sign, "piano teacher," around the corner on Polk Street. So she went up, and it was fifty cents a half hour. So for a dollar we could both have a half-hour lesson every week. We would go together. She would teach one of us, and the other one would sit there. So you learned a little bit from what she was telling the other one.

But very early on the teacher decided that I was the musician and Marge had no talent. Well, you know how it turned out.

When I was in seventh grade Marge and I used to play all kinds of duets—"Little Boy Blue" and "Parade of the Wooden Soldiers." Lots of stuff. We had a lot of fun. But because we didn't take lessons from the sisters, we were never asked to play the march in the school hall.

Marge played everything. She played all the standard songs. She could transpose to different keys. If it was too high for you she could play it lower. She had a notebook with chords. She always had a crowd around her when she played. With me it was . . .

But Ed used to be real nice. On Saturdays we'd be home and Marge would be out somewhere, and he'd say, "Come on. Play the piano, and we'll sing for a while." I'd play as best I could, and he'd sing. It was kind of nice.

One day the sister asked if there was anybody who knew how to play "Parade of the Wooden Soldiers." The girl who was doing the treble part wasn't in school that day. I said I could. She said, Go over to the convent with so-and-so and practice for a little while. So we practiced, and I was thrilled to death that I was going to play in the school hall.

We came out, put up our music, and sat at the piano. The door of the eighth-grade boys' room opened up, and out came Bud McIntyre and two other boys, who said, "What are you doing here?" We said, "We're playing the march." They said, "Who played last week? The girls. It's the boys' turn this week."

I was totally devastated. The big moment in my life, and it was taken away from me just like that by my future brother-in-law.

Getting Hired at Sears

Sears was a few blocks away, at Homan and Arthington. In 1930 half the neighborhood worked there. The girls called it the finishing school, and the boys called it the big house.

The first time I applied, the woman said, "Did you bring your birth certificate?" I gave it to her, and she held it up to the light and said, "I'm sorry, this birth certificate has been tampered with. I can't accept it." So she gave it back to me, and I went home.

My older sister Marge worked downtown, so I decided since she didn't work at Sears I could take her birth certificate. So I went back the very next day, probably wearing the same dress because I didn't have many, and the same woman said, "Did you bring your birth certificate?"

I gave her the birth certificate, and she held it up to the light and said, "OK, here's the application."

So that's how I went to Sears. I had just turned sixteen, and I was scared out of my mind, because I knew that everybody from Providence High School worked there.

The day I started the first person I ran into was my friend Catherine, and I said, "Catherine, can I meet you for lunch?"

She said, "Sure."

I said, "Don't call me anything. Don't tell anyone I'm here until I meet you for lunch." We had macaroni and cheese, which was the best macaroni and cheese I'd ever tasted. I told her my story. "My name is not Jo. I'm Margaret Mary. I didn't know how else to get the job."

She said, "Don't feel so bad. My mother went over to the priest, and he changed my birth certificate for me."

But that's a terrible burden for a kid, to know you're working under an assumed name and there are people who know you from way back. And when is the story going to get around?

From the employment office they sent me to the collection department, and that's the only place I ever worked at Sears. I never left the collection department.

I started as a messenger girl. There were two hundred people at desks, one huge office. You would walk around, and each desk had in and out boxes. You'd drop the stuff that went in and pick up the stuff that was going out.

It so affected me that I used to get up in the middle of the night, take all the blankets off the bed, and fold them up and put 'em on top of a trunk. And my mother would come in—Marge and I slept in the same room—and there would be no covers on either one of us. They'd all be folded up. I was working all day and all night.

I was at Sears about three days and there was another Margaret, another messenger girl. The timekeeper called us out because of the confusion. I said, "Everyone calls me Mary."

She said, "Well, we can call you M. Mary."

But this other Margaret, she said I looked very familiar. She came back after the weekend and said, "I just discovered where I met you. You were at Genevieve's house for a birthday party. And I was talking to Genevieve last night, and she said you must be Jo working as Marge."

I said, "No, I am Marge working as Marge, and you can tell her that." She never said anything else to me about it.

My mother knew that I would be bringing friends from work home, and she immediately started calling me Mary. Rosemarie did too. But my father and Ed and Marge refused totally. My father said, "She's still Jo to me."

One day a group of us from Sears went to lunch at the Aherns', and all through lunch Mrs. Ahern is calling me Jo. On the way back to work one of the girls asked me about it. I said, "Well, that's what my father always called me. I guess he wanted a boy." See, you have to always be ready when you're a fraud.

Penny Postcard

The postcard came on Christmas Eve, 1919. My mother went to the mailbox. She was carrying Rosemarie, who was about six months old. She got the postcard out of the mailbox, and she read it. She started to cry, and she was walking up and down and up and down the house crying. And I'm holding on to the back of her apron, following her up and down the house.

The card was from her stepmother in St. Louis. It was written in pencil with a penny stamp on it, saying, "I'm sorry to tell you that my dear husband and your father died October 24." There was something about how she was so brokenhearted about it. But why didn't she let her know sooner?

Now my mother's real mother had died when she was twelve years old, and not long after, her father remarried. His new wife insisted that my mother go to work, so her father, Patrick Hennessy, went down to his friend Mr. Copelin at the Copelin Studios on Dearborn Street and asked if he could put her to work. My mother was thirteen or fourteen years old. She quit St. Patrick's several months before the end of the eighth grade. But they gave her her diploma.

She worked at Copelin for eleven years, until she got married. She had to quit when she got married. Married women didn't work.

My mother never got along with her stepmother. She said people in the neighborhood used to call the new wife the "Black Widow." People were upset about her father remarrying so soon after his wife had died.

Patrick Hennessy worked for a stove company, and after he remarried he moved to St. Louis to become president of the company. He would keep in touch with my mother with cards and letters. And he'd come visit us when he was in town, with this little fur hat on top of his head and this little mustache. That's how I always remember my grandfather—a tall man with a mustache and a black fur hat.

My mother had always thought he was very well fixed. He'd always had a good job, and he always sent her money. That's how she found out he was dead. She wrote to him the beginning of December, because he always wrote around Thanksgiving and sent money to buy things for the kids for Christmas.

When she didn't get a letter and she didn't get any money, she wrote and asked if he was well. And this penny postcard was in response to her letter. I still have the card.

Ma got somebody's brother, a new lawyer, to go to St. Louis and see about her father's will or his possessions. The lawyer came back and said there was nothing.

During the Depression when things were tough, my father would be slightly inebriated and he would say to my mother, "If you hadn't got that punk lawyer to go to St. Louis for you, if you'd hired somebody worthwhile, you'd have got something out of it and we wouldn't be in this position today."

Grandfather, Patrick Hennessy.

Ghost Story

Cousin Nancy was telling us ghost stories once, and my father heard and said, "Don't believe a word of this. There's always something material behind it. Now, I'll tell you a ghost story."

And he told us how his mother died when he was young and he quit school after third grade and stayed home to take care of the house. One day, after his father went to work, he combed his sister Anna's hair and sent her off to school with the others. And then he was alone in this old farmhouse, in the kitchen washing dishes. And there was a knock, knock, knock, and he opens the door and there's nobody there. And then this happened again. Knock, knock, knock, and no one was there. And then the third time he heard it he said, "Oh, that must be the ghost of my mother."

And so he went outside and walked around the house. He sort of relished the feeling of his mother being there with him. Then he heard knock, knock, knock, and he looked up at the side of the house and the old washtub was banging in the wind.

Rosemarie's Ring

One day we were walking to school and Marge was wearing a ring. I said, "Where'd you get that ring?"

And Marge said, "This is Rosemarie's ring. Ma had it in a glass dish. If you won't say anything, I'll let you wear it this afternoon."

But when we went home for lunch she was panic-stricken because when they passed the wastebasket and she threw her garbage in, the ring fell in too, and she didn't have the nerve to ask to look in the wastebasket. So she said, "Meet me after school and we'll go down to the janitor's room and we'll find it."

So here we are, we're in second and third grade and the garbage box is over our heads, as big as a room. And here we two kids are in the box, up to our ears in paper, trying to find this little ring. But we couldn't find the ring. We stayed there as long as we could, otherwise we'd have to account for our time.

So we went home and Marge made me promise that I'd never say anything about the ring.

Years later, we were all married, one day we were sitting around talking and Ma says, "You know, there's something I've never been able to figure out. Rosemarie had a little ring that her godmother gave her when she was baptized. I know that I had it in a glass dish on the buffet. When we moved I couldn't find it, and that's always puzzled me."

And Marge and I looked at each other and then we both laughed. And I said, "We're too big, she can't do anything now." So we told her the story of what had happened to the ring.

Anyway, that story has always helped me to realize that children do not tell their parents everything.

Mary Jo Hennessy

A very beautiful girl came to our office one day at Sears. Her name was Mary Jo Hennessy. She worked in a different department but she came to the collection department for something and then I would sometimes see her walking down the hallway and I would think, Mary Jo Hennessy, what a beautiful name. Now Hennessy was my mother's maiden name. And I was working under my sister's name, Margaret Mary, but my real name was Josephine and a lot of people called me Jo. My confirmation name was Mary, so if I just took Mary and put it in front I'd have Mary Jo Ryan. Hey, that doesn't sound bad.

I decided that someday I would change my name, so when I started night school at Austin High I registered as Mary Jo Ryan. And Vince went home to his friends after he knew me a while and told them about this girl Mary Jo Ryan, and his cousin Lenore said, "That's too pretty. It almost sounds fictitious."

I never got to know Mary Jo Hennessy but she came through our way once.

The Summer of '41

We used to go up to Lake Delavan in Wisconsin every now and then and rent a cottage.

Once we invited all of our friends. There must have been forty people there for the weekend. Can you imagine that? We had my mother and father come with to do some of the work and to chaperon.

My mother wanted to know what the kids would want to eat. I said, "Oh, baked beans, and hamburgers and hot dogs—stuff like that."

She said, "Well, I'm not going to spend the whole weekend baking beans." She used to bake beans from scratch. You'd take the navy beans and soak 'em all night—and soak 'em and soak 'em. And then you'd cook 'em and cook 'em and put stuff in 'em. So that weekend she decided that she would buy canned beans, and she would put the stuff in that she usually put in, bacon and onions and whatnot. So she did that. The beans were a hit, and she never started from scratch again. Neither do I, and I'm the bean queen.

We spent the whole three days there, and everybody paid three dollars. It was three dollars for the weekend. That bought all the food and all the refreshments—pop and stuff, ice cream.

Then when the weekend was over everybody went home, except for a few of us who stayed there for the rest of the week. We had the whole week's vacation for three dollars.

It was a great time. People slept in their cars and on the front lawn and upstairs and downstairs.

The last time we were there was the summer of '41. It might have been the Fourth of July.

We were all going to come back the next year, but then we never did. The war came. I didn't get back there until 1980. It was amazing how it all looked the same.

Fourth Birthday

I remember my fourth birthday. Lillian and my Aunt Nell Hennessy took me downtown. This would have been 1918.

They took me down to the Boston Store, which was at State and Madison. They got my hair cut and bought me a pair of black patent leather shoes and a box of candy, these beautiful pieces of candy that were made to look like fruit, oranges and strawberries.

On the way home Lillian was practically in tears. "Your mother's going to kill me because I let him cut all your curls."

We walked in the house, Happy Birthday all around, and my mother says, "Lillian, what's wrong?"

She said, "Maud, I hope you don't mind, but I cut off all Jo's curls."

And my mother said, "Jo, come over here." And I went over to the sink and she sprinkled water on my hair and my curls were all there and she wasn't at all mad.

I put on my new black patent leather shoes and my mother gave me a note to go to the butcher shop, which was down the street a ways. And I can remember standing in the butcher shop with my new shoes, making circles in the sawdust.

Aunt Nell Hennessy

In 1919, when I was five years old, I got whooping cough and almost died. I remember my mother sleeping with me every night. We lived in—well, we called it an English basement. Now they'd call it a garden apartment. And my mother used to go to the window in the pitch dark and lift up the window to take the milk in, and the milkman would say, "How is she today?"

I remember that. I mean, you knew when people were saying you were going to die. And somehow or other you knew what that meant.

My Aunt Nell Hennessy brought me a doll buggy when the spring came so that I could put my doll in it, and I would go outside and walk around the yard, because they couldn't get me out of the house and I was supposed to have fresh air. And I would walk around with it once and want to go back inside.

Aunt Nell was always bringing gifts. And my mother would say, "Nell, save your money."

She'd always say, "When I have no money, I'll go to the poor-house." And that's what she did.

Whenever she gave us anything, I always got the top one and my sister Marge got the second-rate. This is from the time we were real little.

Aunt Nell gave us a lot of things. She bought my First Communion dress for me. It was all ruffles, just beautiful. But my mother bawled her out for spending so much money on it.

Aunt Nell said, "Well, I think she should have the best."

And Ma said, "Who do you think is going to iron all these ruffles?" Because you didn't just wash things and hang them up back then. Everything you wore you had to iron. You ironed every ruffle.

So Aunt Nell said, "Well, Maud, take it back and get what you want."

So my mother took it back to the Fair Store and she bought two dresses alike. They were beautiful white dresses. I wore mine for my First Communion, and then Marge and I each had a fancy dress to wear on Sunday. On Sunday, when you got dressed up you stayed dressed all day. You didn't take your fancy clothes off because you came home from church. It was still Sunday.

Aunt Nell also gave us these beautiful dolls. I remember that mine had blond hair and Marge's had black hair. Of course blond was much better than black, so I got the better doll.

When we grew up a little bit, she gave us brown leather purses. They were kidney shaped and they were genuine leather, not brown but sort of a tan, a pretty leather color. We each got one.

Aunt Nell was a cook. She worked the night shift at Effinger's restaurant in the Loop. I have a picture of her standing behind the counter. I remember her singing "Baa, Baa, Black Sheep" to me. That was her favorite song.

She used to come visit us in the morning on the way home from work. She would sit at the table with her hat on. My mother would say, "Nell, take your hat off." And she'd say, "Well, it's about time, I gotta be going."

So one day Aunt Nell's sitting there and Marge, who's only a year older than me, said, "Aunt Nell, don't you think it's about time you gotta be going?"

She said, "Your mother put you up to that!" And she left. She didn't come back to our house for two years.

Now, I didn't know anything about Aunt Nell's past. I just knew that she was somebody who loved me and I loved her. But one day when I was about thirteen or fourteen, we were all gathered around, talking about this and that, and I said, "I've always thought it was such a shame that Aunt Nell never had any children."

Then Ma told me the story about Aunt Nell's children, and I was just devastated. I couldn't believe that this woman I loved so much had given her children away.

See, Aunt Nell had had three husbands. They all died. Sounds funny, doesn't it? People didn't divorce in those days. They died and you got another one.

When her first husband died she had four children, and there was no way she could support them. Her sister had a rooming house, and she said, "You can come and live and work in the rooming house but you can only bring one child."

So Aunt Nell put three of the kids up for adoption and my grandfather Patrick Hennessy, my mother's father, adopted the oldest boy and sent him to school in Canada. Later he flipped a train coming back to Chicago, fell under the wheels, and was killed.

Aunt Nell Hennessy (left) at Effinger's Restaurant.

Aunt Nell kept one child, a girl named Olive. But Olive got sick and died when she was seventeen. So all Aunt Nell's children were gone.

I had another Aunt Nell, Aunt Nell Havern on my mother's side. She was sort of a fancy lady. Aunt Nell Hennessy was the exact opposite.

One day about 1920, Aunt Nell Havern saw an ad in the *Tribune* from a man who was about to get married. "I know I'm adopted," the ad said, "and I'd like to find my own mother." Aunt Nell Havern looked at the picture that was with the ad and recognized it. She called him. He was living in Kenosha, Wisconsin, and she told him if he could tell her something about himself she thought she knew who his mother was. His name was Bobby V——. So she gave the information to Aunt Nell Hennessy.

I don't know if he came down here and met her first, but I do remember when Rosemarie was about a year old, the whole family, Ma, Pa, us four kids, and Aunt Nell all took the train and went to Kenosha to meet him and his adopted family. But I didn't really know who he was until years later when my mother told the story.

Aunt Nell always threw her money around. She was famous for that. She bought Rosemarie a quilted jacket and blanket set for the trip. I remember it as the most gorgeous thing.

Anyway, I know Aunt Nell kept in touch with her son for a while. I have some letters that his adopted mother wrote. But I don't know what happened with him. I know he knew who his sister was. They'd been adopted at the same time. He went to his sister and told her, "I've found our mother." And she said, "No, you haven't. My mother is right here."

One day Aunt Nell lost her job at the restaurant. "I'm going out to the poorhouse," she said. And she did. The poorhouse was in Oak Forest. We used to take the train out to visit her. She sat out there for quite a few months.

Then Cousin Nancy came to our house and she said to my mother, "Maud, where's your Aunt Nell? Father Reynolds at St. Finbarr's lost his cook and he needs a cook. Now, she's a good cook."

"She's sitting out in Oak Forest."

"Well, you go out there and tell her that this is a job for her."

We all went out on the train and she was sitting in her rocker. When we gave her the news she jumped up and got her bag and her clothes and got on the train and came back. It was a big day.

St. Finbarr's was at Harding and 14th Street. Aunt Nell worked there for quite a number of years. We used to love to go and visit her. Marge and I would go on the streetcar. She'd make chocolate cake and she'd make more frosting than she could possibly put on the cake.

When Father Reynolds went duck hunting, she would call us up and tell us to come over, she had a couple of ducks for us. She'd have 'em stuffed and all ready to cook. My mother loved those.

Aunt Nell made all kinds of friends working at St. Finbarr's. They had carnivals galore in those days, and there would be big baskets of food, big hams, lots of handiwork, and beautiful dolls in the booths. You'd put your dime or quarter on a number and they'd spin the wheel and you'd stand there, everybody'd stand there, waiting for the wheel to stop to see who gets the prize. It was great.

I still go to church carnivals but they don't have fun like that anymore. Now you pick tickets out of a bowl. Who cares who wins?

Eventually Father Reynolds died and a new pastor came and he brought his own cook with him. Aunt Nell got a job taking care of Cassie, who lived on Jackson Boulevard. We used to walk out there to visit.

Cassie always carried a purse with her. She was an old lady, a little senile. She was nice but she didn't know what was going on. She carried her purse in the house.

That job lasted for several years and then Cassie died. So Aunt Nell went to the Little Sisters of the Poor. It was on Harrison Street, down near the French church, Notre Dame, two blocks east of there down near Racine.

The old ladies used to wear black dresses, almost like uniforms, and little bonnets on their heads. These were the residents. That's how Aunt Nell looked when I would go visit her. Sometimes I would be the only visitor in this large room.

During the summer I would go every Thursday, and the rest of the year I always went on Sunday. That was my job in the family, go visit Aunt Nell. I would get on the Harrison streetcar and go down there. I think she was there by the time I was thirteen. She died there.

She worked in the laundry. She ironed all those stiff white things that the nuns wore, in the hottest days of summer, no fans or air conditioning. That's what she did for years. The last year of her life, she spent a whole year making capes, white woolen capes. She was knitting them for these sisters that were coming from France to visit. They knew a year in advance that these nuns were coming, so they put her to work making these capes for them.

She worked there. She didn't get anything for free. It wasn't like the poorhouse, where she sat in the rocking chair.

She died about 1932. On Thanksgiving Day I went down to

visit her and I brought her a plate of food. Now, Aunt Nell loved to eat. She was quite a chubby woman. But this time she didn't want to look at the food. She was lying in the bed there. It was like a dormitory, with curtains between the beds.

Aunt Nell was holding on to the curtain, and she said, "Do you realize that I'm dying and you're the only person in the whole world who cares?"

When I got home and my father heard that she wouldn't look at the food, he said, "She must be dying."

They called the next day, Friday, and said she was very sick and that if we wanted to come visit we could, even though it wasn't a visiting day. So my mother went down to see her. I think I went down at the same time. That was the last time I saw her.

A few days later they called and they said she had died, and that they had to get her out of there right away. So they called the undertaker, and he picked her up and then called us. He said she had blown up so big that she couldn't be embalmed. "So we'll make a box this morning and we'll have the funeral this afternoon." She was probably in her seventies by this time. I was about eighteen.

Ma called all the relatives, and we all met at the undertaker's in the afternoon. This was at Ogden and Harrison. The building is still there.

They had her in this plain wooden box, and they'd put some fancy white stuff inside to try and make it look like a regular casket. Aunt Nell looked gigantic, just gigantic. A lot of the relatives hadn't seen her in a long time. Her son wasn't there. I think she must have lost touch through the years.

They closed up the box. They nailed it up and we went out to Mount Carmel Cemetery and she was buried in a lot that belonged to the Little Sisters of the Poor.

Ed was in the seminary at the time, and Ma had called up over there and Father Srill and two or three of the boys came in their cassocks to bless the grave and say a prayer, since we couldn't take her to church or anything.

Anyway, the grave was too small. So we all stood there while they redug the grave. There were all these people standing there, and I knew that none of them, or very few of them, really cared a heck of a lot, and I absolutely refused to cry. I said, I'm not going to make a . . . out of this, and my mother wasn't crying. It didn't seem like anybody was crying, and I wasn't going to cry.

After the funeral we went home and I went down to the basement to be alone. So I could cry where nobody would see me. I found my mother down there and she was doing the same thing. So there's the two of us bawling over Aunt Nell down in the basement, crying on each other's shoulders.

When she went to the Sisters of the Poor, before she left, Aunt Nell bought us each a lovely watch, Marge and me, "so that we would remember her." I still have it somewhere, one of my souvenirs.

She always wanted to be remembered.

Better Late Than Early

When I first met Vince, he was working in this solder factory, somewhere around 22nd and Indiana. I used to meet him on the corner by the Lexington Hotel at 22nd and Michigan. Is that still there?

He used to like to tell the story of how he got this job. One day he saw an ad in the paper for a laborer—this was 1937. So he was planning to apply. But he slept late, and when he got up he took his time and had breakfast. When he's finally ready to go, it's about noon and his mother is berating him. She said, "You'll never get a job if you don't go early."

But he goes anyway, and the man interviewed him. Then he asked him, "Can you lift a hundred pounds?" Because he had to lift these big blocks of solder. They made the solder, and they poured it into molds. It was heavy work and hot work.

Vince says yes, he can lift a hundred pounds.

The man says, "Well, you've got the job. I had 175 people here this morning. Now I can't remember who's who."

There'd been a line of people down the block in the morning, and he had applications all over his desk. But now he couldn't remember which face went with which name. So he hired Vince. And Vince went home and told his mother that he got the job because he came late.

Day of Glory

At Sears I started as a messenger girl in the collection department, but pretty soon they recognized my talents. I got a promotion. I became a typist.

My friend Catherine became a typist too. But she typed "you owe us's." That was when somebody owed less than a dollar. She would type like a hundred of these notices an hour. All she had to do was type the name and address and fill in the amount, but the thing was, she had to get the names and everything from the envelopes that the order had come in. So she became an expert at reading these crazy handwritings.

I typed letters, collection letters, and all I did was type names and addresses too. But I had files that I typed from rather than just envelopes. I was a good typist, so one day they promoted me again.

Catherine, with her experience, became a statistical typist. She typed these long sheets with numbers all the way across, and she was perfect at it.

I typed legal cards—for every case in the legal department there was a card. And they were so pleased with my improving the legal cards that one day I was asked to be the typing supervisor.

All the typing from all over the department went through my desk, and I would look at it and make sure it was OK. My day of glory came when I found a "skip-tracing" letter going to Highland Park. I recognized the name—it was the chairman of the board of Sears. The letter was asking him if he could furnish the address of a woman who had been in his employ who owed Sears some money.

Well, I gave the letter to my supervisor, Miss Krueger, and she was delighted, so she took it to the manager, Mr. Vale. He thought this was wonderful, that he had been saved the embarrassment of sending this letter out to the chairman of the board.

I was out on a ten-minute break. When I got back Miss Krueger came over to me and said, "Guess who came to visit you? Mr. Vale stood at your desk for eleven minutes. Breaks are ten, you know. He wanted to congratulate you on having found that letter." So he never did congratulate me. But I was told he wanted to, so that was my big deal.

Pleurisy

⤮

My mother got sick when I was in eighth grade. We were all going to church, Ma and the four kids. It was December 8, 1927. The Feast of the Immaculate Conception, a holy day. When we got to the corner of Harrison and Albany she said, "I've got to go home. I have a pain in my chest. You kids go on to mass."

So she went home and she went to bed, and she never got out of bed until Easter Sunday. She had pleurisy.

She was in bed for all those months. At first I stayed home from school and did what I could for her. About the middle of January we got Mrs. Ahern, who lived two doors down, to stay with her, and I went back to school.

My mother had Dr. Sullivan first. His office was at 12th and Crawford, and he mixed his own medicine. He came to visit her the first time, and I rode back with him. He mixed the medicine and gave me the bottles, and I brought it home. She started taking the medicine, but then after a while she swore the medicine was making her worse.

My father was working on the Stevens Hotel, so he was out till ten o'clock at night. They were working all this overtime trying to finish.

She kept screaming the medicine was killing her. One night she was so bad that I ran next door and asked Mrs. McLaughlin if she could give me the name of her doctor. We called him, and he wasn't available. So then we went to the next house, Mrs. Lally, and she gave me the name of her doctor, Dr. Williams. I called him and he came.

He said, "Well, yes, the medicine is a little too strong." That was all he'd say about it. He took care of her from then on. He didn't mix his own medicine.

She had this ointment she used to rub on her chest. She couldn't breathe. We had to rub this stuff on her all the time. She didn't have any energy.

The funny thing, when she got better she said, "Well, who couldn't make a person well if you stayed in bed all the time?" That's what she thought, that the doctor made her better by keeping her in bed all that time.

I don't know how many times the priest came. Us four kids would kneel on the floor at the foot of the bed, and he would anoint her and give her the last rites. And she would always bounce back.

On Easter she got up. When I think back on that now, it was always in the back of my mind that she was going to die. See, her mother died when she was twelve, and Pa's mother died when he was about twelve.

But my mother got better, and in June I graduated from Our Lady of Sorrows.

Aunt Maggie and Uncle Bill

Aunt Maggie was a housekeeper for a man on the North Side. The man had a little girl named Tillie and sometimes Aunt Maggie would bring her along when she came to visit. *Tillie the Toiler* was a famous comic strip at the time, so we used to call the girl Tillie the Toilet.

One Saturday Aunt Maggie came to stay with us on Flournoy Street. Sunday she went to mass at Our Lady of Sorrows, and when she came out of church, she's walking down Albany Avenue and she sees a man sitting up against a lamppost with his legs twisted under him and his hat out and she recognized him. It was her employer, begging. This is how he made all the money he was able to afford a housekeeper with.

So Aunt Maggie quit and came to live with us. She couldn't read, so Pa would look in the paper for jobs and my mother would write letters for her.

A widower in Sycamore needed a housekeeper. So Ma wrote

the letter and he wrote back and said Aunt Maggie should come out. So she took the job and moved out there. And after a couple of years they decided to marry. He became our Uncle Bill. He had five acres, what they called a truck farm.

When they got too old to take care of the farm they got an apartment on Milwaukee Avenue upstairs of a store by Six Corners. And then they both went to the Little Sisters of the Poor, to the nursing home. And he died there. He was buried from the Little Sisters. She must have died there too but I can't remember when. It might have been during the war.

Cancer of the Larynx

Right after we came home from Florida in 1945, my father got sick. He coughed, he coughed, and he coughed. He was sure that he'd gotten tuberculosis from his brother-in-law, who had just died. Pa still smoked. He rolled his own. So eventually he went to the doctor to find out about his TB. It was cancer of the larynx.

He was at the Illinois Research Hospital, and Marge and Ma and I and Aunt Anna went down to see him one night. Aunt Anna told him that he was wasting his time in a research hospital, he should have her doctor in Maywood. So he's putting his coat and hat on when the doctor walks in.

"Where are you going, Mr. Ryan?"

Pa said, "I'm going home. These ladies are dragging me out of here."

The doctor said, "Well, let me tell all of you, if you leave here you won't live more than six months. If you stay you've got a chance."

So Pa took his hat and coat off and stayed.

When he got out of the hospital he had to go for treatments every day, five days a week. He said they put pins in his neck. And his neck was dotted with holes—pin marks. I suppose it was an early form of radiation.

He did that for a whole year. Marge came over every day and took him on the streetcar—maybe by then there were buses—and took him down to the hospital. It was down by County Hospital. It was part of the University of Illinois. Every day he went for almost a year, and then one day he decided he wouldn't go anymore. He couldn't eat. Food never went down.

So then the doctor came out to the house. "What's with you, John, that you're not coming to the hospital?"

My father said, "You're not doing me any good."

The doctor said they could feed him through his stomach. They said that the passage between his throat and his stomach was gone, and so that was the only way they could do it.

Pa said he had had a long life, and it was a good life. And he didn't see any reason why he should have somebody feeding him through his stomach. So he wasn't going to do that. And he didn't.

I walked to the door with the doctor. This was just before Pegge was born. The doctor said to me, "How are you keeping out from under all this?"

I said, "Well, I just do what I have to do. That's all."

He said, "Well, you know your father has cancer?"

I said, "Yes, we know that."

He said, "Well, he won't live very long."

So because I was expecting a baby very soon, Pa and Ma went to Rosemarie's. She lived on Cicero Avenue on the North Side. And that's where he died. It always seemed strange to me that both Ma and Pa died at Rosemarie's. I took care of them most of the time, but they both died at Rosemarie's.

Although I must say I never did much for my father. He always took care of himself. He got up every morning and shaved, took a bath, put a clean shirt on, and then sat down and read the newspaper. On Memorial Day, a few weeks before he died, I helped him take his shoes off. He was going to lie down, and he couldn't take his shoes off. That's the only thing I can ever remember that I did for him personally.

He didn't like going to Rosemarie's. They told him that he could watch the traffic on Cicero Avenue. He said, "What's that?"

Monroe Street was his home, and he felt he was displaced. But everyone felt that I shouldn't be taking care of Ma and Pa when I was expecting in a few weeks. That's why they went in both cases, because I was almost due.

Pegge was born three weeks after my father died, and Mary Jo was born five weeks after my mother died. So I always thought it was a real blessing to have a new baby to take their place. A new joy. You didn't have time to think about how bad you felt.

Austin High and How I Met My Husband

In 1936 I got fifty dollars from Sears as a bonus for their fiftieth year in business. I wanted to buy a used dining-room set for the family, but my mother wouldn't let me. She said I had to spend it on myself, and I wanted something that would last.

So I decided I'd use it to go to school. I read about this place where you could take a three-month course and go to the University of Illinois and take the exam and get high school credits. So I went. I took Latin, economic theory, and some kind of English or something. I got the three high school credits, but I didn't have any more money.

I tried going to Crane High School once, and it was so awful. But now we were living in Austin, so in 1937 I went to Austin High. I took an English literature course two nights a week.

The second night of the course this guy walks in and takes the seat in front of me. He hadn't been in class the first night. So the teacher told him that since he was late, she would like him to write a list of the books he'd read.

So this guy is sitting in front of me, and he starts writing. He's writing. He's writing. He's writing. And I'm thinking, where has he been all his life? How could anybody possibly read all those books? But, you know, he had read and read and read and read. And so he just went on and on, writing down books, author at a time. Class was almost over, and he was still writing.

So one day there in class we were reading something from old literature, and the teacher asked, "What does that refer to?"

A guy in the back of the class said, "That refers to going to confession."

Vince turns back to me like this and says, "Oh, there's a Catholic in the crowd."

I said, "So what?" That's the first thing we ever said to each other.

After that he started to walk with us. I used to meet this whole crowd of girls going home. There was Rosemarie, Anna Mae, and Madeline Carroll, and a couple of others.

The English literature class was in the old building, which was torn down years ago. It was right behind the new building, which wasn't very new even then.

Anyway, one night Vince says to me, "Who are you waiting for?"

I said, "Oh, just a group of girls. We walk home together." They came out, and I introduced him—and he just walked along with us. So every night it was the usual thing that he would walk along with us.

We used to go to the drugstore at Laramie and Madison—this was when we still lived on Jackson. A group of girls going to have a Coke after school. Vince would come in to buy his mother a pack of cigarettes. I would think, gee, he must have a very modern, up-to-date mother, you know, if she smokes.

Anyway, one night on the way to the drugstore he said to me, "How would you like to go roller-skating Sunday?"

Well, I'd never thought about going out with him, and I said, "Oh, no, I don't think so."

He said, "Well, here, take this book and let me know what you think about it." It was *Human Being* by Christopher Morley. I'd like to read it again someday to see what it's like, because I don't remember a word of it.

We all went into the drugstore, and he got his cigarettes for his mother and went home. I sat down at the table and I said, "Vince asked me out."

Anna Mae said, "Oh, when are you going?"

I said, "I'm not going."

She said, "Why not?"

I said, "I don't know. I just don't feel like it."

She said, "Well, I wish he'd asked me."

After we were married we used to go visit Anna Mae's mother every New Year's Day. She liked a dark-haired man to come visit her on New Year's Day. She said it was good luck. And every time we came she'd say, "Vince, why didn't you choose Anna Mae?" It was funny.

So anyway, that's my story of Austin High School and how I met my husband.

New Year's Eve Wake

Vince's mother died a few weeks after Pearl Harbor. She had a stroke. She'd been sick for a while.

She had high blood pressure, and she was desperate because she couldn't get a job. She was all of forty-nine years old, but she was too old to work. She'd always had these really good jobs. She was secretary to the manager of the Century of Progress, and then she was secretary to the editor of the *Chicago Journal of Commerce*. But nobody would hire her anymore.

The wake was on New Year's Eve at Vince's Aunt Agnes's, on the South Side. The whole family was there, and Agnes served wine to everybody. They had a great big living room. This is where Vince's mother was laid out.

It was almost midnight. George, a friend of Vince's mother, was telling a story, and the clocks were ticking—they had one of these big clocks. It struck midnight. Well, George didn't stop telling his story. He kept going straight through to the end. My father had a fit. He didn't stop talking about that for years. He said it was the first time in his life that he ever knew a man who wouldn't stop what he was doing at midnight on New Year's.

The funeral was the second of January, and it was freezing cold. My father was a pallbearer, and he was standing at the grave with his hat in his hand. All the women were saying, "Mr. Ryan, put your hat on."

He said, "I have never stood in the presence of the dead with my hat on, and I won't do it now." He was from the old school.

Gifts Aren't Important

Marge and I wanted roller skates for Christmas, but we got dolls. My mother said Santa Claus thought we were too young for roller skates. We were probably five and six. That same year, Aunt Anna gave us little rosary beads—silver rosary beads in a little silver case with a chain on it. You put your finger through the chain and held the case. Very pretty little thing.

Also, I remember that my mother cried that day. It seemed like she was crying all day. So after I grew up I asked her about it. "Mom, remember that Christmas on Flournoy Street when you cried all day?"

"You remember that? I didn't think you'd even noticed."

I said, "What was it all about?"

"Well, it was a very foolish thing. I've thought many, many times how really stupid that was. I was mad at your father because he gave Aunt Maggie and me the same gift. He gave us each a pound box of the Sampler chocolates."

That's what she was hurt about. So she said, "Gifts aren't that important." See, you learn from other people's mistakes too.

*Confirmation day, 1924, Our Lady of Sorrows. Margaret
(Marge) and Josephine (Mary Jo) Ryan.*

More Will Than Won't

When I first met Vince, he told me that he was twenty and he was only nineteen. And I told him that I was twenty-two but I was twenty-three. So we each knew that we had lied but we didn't know that the other one had too. So we were really four years apart.

Vince was Irish too. We were out with Marge once and she said, "You're not Irish, not with a name like Gantes."

He said, "All I can say is, I have two grandparents that were born in Ireland. How many do you have?" And he knew. We only had one.

When he was a kid he sang in the Holy Name choir and he went to Holy Name School. But most of the time he went to boarding school. From the time he was six. This was because his mother worked. She sent him to the fanciest boarding schools she could afford and he hated 'em all. He said, "If we ever have kids, they'll never go away to school unless they really want to."

He was born in Baltimore and he lived in New York until he was two, then his mother came to Chicago to visit her sister. While she was here, her sister's kids got the measles and then Vince got them too. So she was stuck. She figured she might as well go get a job and do something with her time. She got a job with the *Chicago Journal of Commerce*.

So she liked the job and she decided it was better than the one she had in New York. So they stayed here.

When he wasn't in boarding school or summer camp he lived with his Aunt Agnes somewhere on South Blackstone. Whenever he talked about the good things of his childhood, it was when he was with Aunt Agnes and her six kids.

He went to Marmion High School, a Catholic boarding school. But while he was going it became a military school. So he begged his mother to let him go to New York to school. She had these friends who lived on Long Island.

So he lived out on Manhasset, Long Island, and he went to DePaul High School in Manhattan at night and worked in a gas station during the day. He did that for two years.

He told me a funny story from his New York days. He said he'd be going out on a date with these two other guys and before they'd pick up the girls, the guys would say, "Vince, don't talk politics tonight."

We used to argue a lot about politics in those days.

The reason he came to live on the West Side was for the night school. Austin had a good night school.

We broke up a few times. Once, after we'd broken up, some of us were sitting on the porch on Menard and here comes Vince, up from Columbus Park, eating an ice cream cone. And, you know, we all say, "Hi."

And then he says, "Hi." And then he stopped and stayed for the rest of the evening.

He always said he was glad he had more willpower than I had won't power.

Learning to Ride

When we moved to Flournoy Street, there was a little porch with about three steps down to the sidewalk. So Ed was about four or five. He gets on his tricycle the first day we were there, and he rides off the porch. He split his head open. We had to take him to the doctor for stitches.

Later, when we lived on Arthington Street, someone gave Ed a bike and my mother made him give it away or sell it. She was afraid that he'd get killed on the street.

There weren't many cars in those days but kids weren't very careful. They played baseball and other games in the middle of the street. We used to play all those games, like Red Rover come over and all that stuff, and there was a little boy named Smith who lived down the street, and he was killed by a car.

None of us ever had bikes until we were much older.

After Manley High School was built they widened Sacramento

Boulevard. It was lined with trees and they widened it, took all the trees down, and it became a gasoline highway.

But when they were working on the street, it was quite the fashion to go bike riding. You could rent a bike for twenty-five cents an hour. I didn't know how to ride so my father said, "Come on. We'll go down to Sacramento and I'll show you how." So we went down to the boulevard. I was probably about seventeen.

It's night and there's nobody on the street. The new cement is dry but the street hasn't opened. It was all blocked off. So he's holding the back of the bike while I ride. Gives me a few pointers and then lets go and I'm riding on my own.

So then we would rent bikes. And we would ride over to Garfield Park or Douglas Park. I remember one time in Douglas Park there were about five of us riding together and somebody in the front fell and everybody else fell behind them. We were all down. But nobody was hurt and later we thought it was funny.

Marble Accident

My father was hurt in an accident. This was 1922. He worked in a marble shop somewhere south. They had this machine they used to polish marble. When we went to visit him when we were little kids he would put us on it and make it go around like a merry-go-round.

One day while he was polishing marble, something fell and hit him. He fell into the machine, and the machine threw him around and out on the floor. They found him there and brought him home.

My mother was just getting dressed to take us on a picnic in Garfield Park, which she did many Thursdays. I always remember her with white blouses and long, black skirts. This day she'd put her skirt on, and it was inside out. She said, "Oh, bad luck—I put my skirt on inside out."

That's how kids get these dumb ideas. So she turned the skirt around, and the doorbell rang. She went to the door and there was my father, with two men carrying him. His head was crushed.

They said he had to go for X rays, so my mother sent me running over to get Aunt Maggie, who lived at Van Buren and Kedzie. She came over to watch the kids, and my mother went with my father and these men to the hospital.

He had a brain concussion and a fractured skull. He was forty-nine at the time. Before that he had red hair, but it all fell out. I don't remember if it happened in the hospital or when he got home. But he was almost completely bald for a while. When his hair did grow back, it came in gray. After that he was always gray.

And for the rest of his life he had a ringing in his ears. He used to ask us to please be quiet. He couldn't stand the ringing.

He didn't get any money—not that I know of. He was out of work for a while. I couldn't say how long. I know he was lying on the couch for a long, long time.

Aunt Anna and Uncle Percy

I don't know where Aunt Anna met Uncle Percy. Probably down along Printers Row. The book bindery where she worked as a forelady was on Plymouth Court near Harrison. And he was a printer.

She went with him for seventeen years. He used to write her postcards. You know, you'd put 'em in the box in the morning with a penny stamp, and she would have them the next morning, asking her to meet him at a certain spot after work—and they'd go to a show.

One day in 1918 one of my mother's cousins came to our house and said, "I see your sister-in-law got married yesterday."

"Which one?" my mother asked.

"Anna. I saw her in St. Finbarr's, walking down the aisle."

Now at the time, Aunt Anna was helping take care of her father, Philip Ryan, my grandfather. So when my father came home he went over to the house where his father and sisters lived.

He said, "So you married him?" She admitted it. "Well, dammit, go live with the man. You don't have to stay here."

So Aunt Anna and Uncle Percy moved to a place of their own.

Percy's real name was Patrick. He was a great guy. We loved him. He was so good to us. And he could sing like John Mc-Cormack. He had all of John McCormack's records. They had a beautiful home, beautiful furniture, everything nice, and they treated us royally.

My father gave him the name Percy. This man was very tall and skinny. About six foot three inches. You'd think you could knock him over with a feather. My father would say, "He doesn't drink, smoke, or chew." This was intended as an insult.

Percy went into a bar on a hot Sunday afternoon and found the bartender asleep behind the bar—he used to love to tell this story himself. He tapped on the bar, and the bartender finally woke up. "What can I do for you?"

Percy said, "I'd like a tall glass of ice-cold milk."

The bartender said, "Sonny, the day nursery is right around the corner." And he went back to sleep.

After a couple of years they bought a house in Maywood. There were no sidewalks, no streets. It was a white stucco house, and it was beautiful. It was just like a dollhouse, and that's where he got sick. He had consumption, TB.

They weren't in the house six months and he got sick. She had ultraviolet-ray machines, and nurses day and night, and all that sort of stuff for him. But he wasn't getting any better.

She had a cousin living in California. She had a great big back porch in Pasadena, lots of fresh air. She told Aunt Anna, the thing to do is come to California. So they closed up the house and gave my mother and father the key to take care of it for them.

They stayed in California for maybe two or three years, but Percy wasn't any better. So they came back, opened their house in Maywood, and Aunt Anna got her job back at the book bindery.

She used to take the Toonerville Trolley from 17th Avenue in Maywood to Austin and Madison, and then she'd get the street-car downtown. The trolley was a single car with straw seats, and it had a big coal stove in the back. That's how they kept the car warm in the winter.

We went out to Maywood for every holiday. They couldn't go anywhere, so every holiday we went there. If you went out the door you'd hear her: "Don't slam that door." Or if you closed it quietly, she'd say, "Don't let the flies in."

She was always tough like that. But she was a very responsible person. She worked and took care of people all her life.

I used to try to make her talk about when she was young. "Tell me what it was like when you were young." And I would like to have gotten some answers about Uncle Percy, why she went with him for all those years. But all she'd say was, "I found out a long time ago that you never get in trouble if you keep your mouth shut." And that was all she'd tell me.

Uncle Percy sat and read his books and studied Latin and chatted with the minister who lived across the street. They used to have wonderful conversations. Percy was Catholic. This minister was Presbyterian. One day he said to Percy, "You know, I'd join your church, but I'd be out of a job if I did."

I think that's what got my father in the end. Uncle Percy sat there and read his books and talked to the minister and studied this and that while my father ran to Maywood and fixed the roof and fixed the windows and put up the storms. And Percy did nothing. He just sat. He was so skinny that you couldn't tell if he was really sickly.

My father was kind of a comic, but he was a critic too. He always said, "When Percy dies it won't be from TB." And it wasn't. He died in 1945 of stoppage of the heart. He was about sixty-two.

Also Known as Josephine Agnes and Mike Gantes

When I met him his name was Vincent M. Gantes. But he said call him Mike, which was his middle name. That went on until one Christmas Eve when he asked me to walk over to Lake and Austin. He said, "I want to go visit this friend of mine, Alice. She has a rental library." They rented books.

So we walked through the snow, and when we walked in the door someone in the back says, "Oh, is that you Vincent?"

He says, "Oh, mother, I didn't know you were gonna be here." He knew very well she was going to be there.

That's how I met his mother. She was very nice. She said to me, "Do you call him that terrible Mike name?"

I said, "Oh, no. I call him Michael."

She said, "I call him Vincent."

So when we walked out of there I said, "Vincent, that's your name." I called him that ever after.

Now, we knew each other quite a long time, a couple of years,

*With Vince in 1940, after we graduated from Austin
night school.*

and one day he says to me, "I have something very important I have to tell you."

I thought, my God, what's this?

He said, "My name really isn't Vincent Gantes."

And I said, "What's so funny about that? Mine isn't really Mary Jo Ryan."

He was really amazed.

So now he told me that his name was Vincent Clark. That his father, Clark, was a newspaper man and he'd died in the flu epidemic before he was born or shortly thereafter, and that his mother had remarried Gantes, and so for her convenience she called him Vincent Gantes so she wouldn't have to be explaining him everywhere.

And then, of course, I explained how I got my name, which was a funnier story than how he got his. He liked my story. He was really floored though.

Oh, and then I went home and told my mother, "His name is not Gantes. It's Clark." She was the happiest woman in the world. By this time she'd decided I was going to marry him. She didn't want me to have a name like Gantes. I think she thought it was too foreign sounding.

Current Events

Aunt Maggie came to live with us in 1924. Now, she was a very intelligent woman, but she couldn't read or write. My father would read the newspaper to her, all the special articles. The next day you'd hear her telling somebody about some important thing that happened yesterday. "It was in the *Daily News,* you know." And she couldn't read a word. But nobody knew that except the family. That was a secret.

We weren't allowed to read the newspaper when we were little. My father always ranted and raved about the *Herald Examiner.* The *Daily News* was his paper, but we kids couldn't read it.

So in class, in fifth grade, I was to do current events. I wasn't allowed to read the newspapers, but I grabbed one and got the fastest thing I could find. And when it was my turn I stood up and said, "A woman is suing her husband for divorce because he's bald." The sister said, "Now wait a minute. That is not a current event." She said, "We'll give you another chance next week."

So next Wednesday I'd been able to grab a look at the paper again, and I stood up and said, "Jackie Coogan went to visit the pope."

One of my classmates jumped up and said, "Oh, you're always talking about movie stars and things like that, and that's not current events."

The sister said, "I beg to differ. That's a very good current event, that Jackie Coogan went to visit the pope."

"We Are Talking About Your Attendance"

When you worked at Sears, you worked. Maybe that's why a lot of people are such good workers, because they always had to work so hard.

Anyway, in 1940 I ended up in the collection department sitting next to Chuck Hanna. We dictated letters. We did all the no-payment accounts, where people would buy something and not even make the first payment. We were the guys who wrote the letters, sent out the stuff to the collectors.

Hanna used to teach me things, things he had learned in college. Every day he would write something out for me. He knew I was going to Loyola at night.

I had never been to college before—I had just finished high school. And he knew all this stuff that I didn't know—definitions of words, philosophy, and all kinds of stuff.

Then Mr. Hanna, he couldn't afford to work at Sears anymore. He was making about thirty-five dollars a week. I was making twenty-three.

He had three kids, and he was expecting the fourth. He gave up smoking. He said, "I can't afford to buy cigarettes."

So then he went out looking for a job. What he would do, he'd bring a suit coat and a shirt and leave it in the car. And then his wife would call and say one of the kids was sick or something, and he'd run out, get in the car, run over to the park somewhere, change his clothes, and then go for the interview. Anyway, he got a job at Spiegel's.

So I got his job. When he left I was doing what he had done. After I'd had the job for about four months I was called into the manager's office, and he says to me, "I called you in to tell you that I want you to improve your attendance." I didn't know what he was talking about.

He said, "You have been tardy four times in the past year."

I didn't miss a day. I was never late. But I had been tardy four times. Eight o'clock was the starting time, but you were supposed to be there by 7:55. If you got there by 7:55 you were on time. But if you got there at 7:56 you were tardy. If you got there after 8 you were late.

You should have seen my friend Catherine and me running up five flights of stairs to punch in. *Now,* if she punched in first she could be 7:55 and I could be 7:56. But anyway, four times in a whole year I got there after 7:55 but before 8.

So I listened, and I said, "I'm sorry. I'll try to do better."

Then I said, "By the way, I have taken over Mr. Hanna's job for four months now, and I haven't received any raise in pay."

He said, "Miss Ryan, we are not talking about the work you do today. We are talking about your attendance. Good day." How do you like that?

Jackson Park Bridge

It was my mother who noticed that Vince had a glass eye.

And she said to me, "Mary, if you get involved with him, you might end up having a blind husband. Because if one eye is bad, the other one might go too."

My mother was looking out for my welfare. She liked Vince. She saw he had a lot of good qualities. But she was very much afraid that I would marry a blind man and she didn't want me to get started on him.

I said, well, I didn't think he would be blind and we weren't thinking of marriage, anyway.

And she said, "That's how these things start. Don't get into it and you won't have to worry about it."

It wasn't that she didn't like him. She admired him, his going to school and working full time. She was concerned for me.

One day I was to meet Vince by the Lexington Hotel, but he

didn't come. So I went around the corner to this restaurant and had lunch. It must have been a Saturday.

After lunch I came back and stood around the hotel again, and then walked around the block. Vince was always a very on-time person. He never stood me up, that's for sure. So I knew that there must be something wrong.

Finally around two o'clock he came. He apologized and said he was surprised to find me still there. And I said, "Well, where else would I go to meet you." And that was it. He didn't know where else to go to meet me either, except where we had made the arrangements.

He said. "Let's go out to Jackson Park." So we took the bus. We had a spot there by a bridge where we used to sit and talk. So we went to our spot and sat down. And he took an eye patch out of his pocket and said, "Do you know what I do with this?" And I said, "Yes, you wear it when you take your eye out." And he said, "So you know." And I said, "Yes."

Then he told me that when he was cleaning the eye that morning he dropped it on the bathroom floor and it broke in a million pieces. So he had to go downtown to the eye place to get a new one. And it had taken longer than he thought. That's where he'd been. And then he told me the story of how he'd lost his eye.

He'd been shot with a BB gun when he was ten. He'd been playing with a bunch of boys behind this athletic club that used to be on Chicago Avenue east of Michigan.

He couldn't see out of the eye and it was very disfigured. He used to wear glasses with one dark lens.

His mother didn't want him to get a glass eye. She said eventually they would have a way of fixing his eye, and now they would. They have these implants and stuff. She thought if he would just hold on eventually there would be something that would give him his sight back.

But he got tired of wearing the glasses, making excuses. So when he was nineteen and living in New York, he made up his mind to get an artificial eye. So he came back to Chicago and got his eye removed and went to Austin night school, and that's where I met him soon after.

St. James at Sag Bridge

My grandfather Philip Ryan died in November 1924, when I was ten. He was eighty-nine. I remember going to visit him when he was sick. He was wrapped in a blanket, sitting in his chair.

He was waked at home. They had these red candles on either side of the casket, and we kids—there were six of us—we stayed all night. We laid crosswise in the bed so there was enough room, and I was on the end and could look out through the brass rails of the bed and see the lights flickering on the open casket. In the morning we got up early, and all the kids went in and we said the Rosary.

People were in the kitchen smoking and eating and drinking. An Irish wake.

This was the first funeral I remember. He was buried from Our Lady of Angels Church on Hamlin Avenue. The funeral procession went out Archer Avenue to St. James the Sag near Lemont. The trees were all covered with snow and ice.

When we got to the Sag, the Ryans from the farm were there—Philip's nieces and nephews who lived out that way. They opened the casket so they could say good-bye.

So when I go out to the Sag and I think of where these people are buried, I can picture just where Philip Ryan is, because that's where the casket was opened. Strange.

My great-grandfather, Thomas McLaughlin, is also buried there, alongside his two wives, Mary and Margaret.

Margaret was Irish, and the story was that her family had fixed her up to marry some English nobleman. But he wasn't Catholic, and he wanted her to join his church. So she fled to America, where she holed up in this little church near Lemont thinking she'd be safe—and along came Thomas McLaughlin.

Now sometime after his wife died in 1855, Thomas McLaughlin went to get the priest for his son, who was dying. Margaret, who was the housekeeper at the rectory, answered the door. She told him the priest wasn't in, and he told her why he was there. She said, "Well, wait. He'll be back soon." She took his coat and his hat and all that stuff. The fire was on, and he sat in front of the fireplace.

And she went out to the kitchen and made him a plate of bread and eggs—fried eggs—and whatnot.

Well, forty-five minutes later, when the priest came back, they asked him to marry them. So before he went to see the dying son, the priest married them.

Margaret got in the wagon with them and went to the farm. And as she was getting out of the wagon, it occurred to her to wonder if the dying son was the only child, and then she found he had all these other children.

Anyway, Cousin Nancy said she was a wonderful mother to

all those children. She never had any of her own. And she was a wonderful grandmother.

Now Thomas McLaughlin died in 1873, and Margaret lived on quite a long time. They're all buried at the Sag—Thomas McLaughlin and both wives, Margaret and Mary—right in front of the church.

About ten years ago somebody smashed Thomas McLaughlin's tombstone. The historical society out there paid to put the stone back together. They put a new front on it. It was beautiful. And then a few years ago the vandals were out again, and this time they smashed Mary McLaughlin's stone too. I should really do something about getting them repaired.

Why do people do these crazy things?

Uncle Jim

Uncle Jim—now that's quite a story. He never married. I think he had a live-in lady at one time. But anyway, he was an elevator installer. He worked for Otis Elevator. He was living in a rooming house by himself, and he would keep in touch with Aunt Anna, call her up occasionally.

Anyway, one day in 1944 she realized that she hadn't heard from him for a long time. So she called my mother and asked her if she would go with her to this rooming house, to see if he was OK. So they went. They knew the number of the house, but they didn't know who owned it. They knocked on the door, and a woman answered. They asked for Jim Ryan.

"Oh, Jim Ryan," the woman said. "He died several months ago." She said they didn't know he had any relatives.

They called our friend Smith, the undertaker, and he looked into it and found that he'd been buried in a potter's field in Oak Forest. And that was my Uncle Jim.

I had just moved to Florida in March. This must have been April. During Easter I worked at this florist. I got a letter about Uncle Jim—how they'd found him in a potter's field, and they'd dug him up, and he was going to be buried on Good Friday. They were bringing him out to the Sag. I remember going to the church across the street from the florist on Orange Avenue at the time of the funeral and saying a prayer for him.

St. Nicholas's Day

When my mother was an invalid, I used to tell her how lucky we were that we'd had her all those years. I always remembered when she was sick when I was in eighth grade. She'd had pleurisy, and it was always in the back of my mind that she was going to die. We could have lost her back then. But we didn't.

We went on a vacation in the summer of '51, and we left Ma with Rosemarie. Pa was already gone. He'd died in '48. And when we came back, Rosemarie wouldn't let Ma come home. She said, "Your kids have had the advantage of her all these years, and my kids should get a chance."

That was in August. Aunt Anna's birthday was in November, and we agreed that Ma was to come home then. But she didn't come home. She didn't feel very good.

A few days later, Vince went down to Springfield to get his law license. When he came home, he went over to Rosemarie's

Ma with some of her grandchildren, summer of 1951. (Back row, left to right) Mary Jude and Peggy Ryan, Maudemarie, Vincent, Pegge Clark, and Tom McLaughlin. (Front row) Pat McLaughlin (sitting) and Jack Clark (standing).

to show Ma his license. And she admired his new blue serge suit. Anyways, it was only a few days later that she died.

I stayed with her the night before. And the next morning, Vince brought the kids over. We had Maude, Vincent, Peg, and Jack. Yeah, four. You were the youngest. She loved you. You were about a year and a half. And we had a couple of candles burning on the dresser and we told the kids that the candles were to light Grandma's way to heaven.

Vince took the kids home and Mrs. Murphy and Mrs. Trier went over to take care of them.

Marge and Rosemarie; Ed was there too. 1951. She died on St. Nicholas's Day, the sixth of December.

Father Miller and Father Mulherin

Everybody in the neighborhood went to Our Lady of Sorrows. The priests would walk down the street on summer days and there were always kids playing outside, and Father Mulherin and Father Miller were two very gregarious priests. They would see kids and if they didn't know 'em, they'd ask where they went to school. They'd look at their Irish face and know they should be Catholic and they'd say, "Go in and get your mother. Tell her I want to talk to her." And the mother would come out, and the kid would be in Our Lady of Sorrows the next year. Tuition was only fifty cents a month. But the tuition wasn't important. Every Catholic child had to be in the Catholic school. So they didn't care whether the tuition got paid or not. A lot of kids went to school free.

Loyola University: He Went North and I Went West

Vince and I graduated from Austin in June 1940, and then we went to register at Loyola University. I had this idea of this great university I was going to attend, and then we walked into this dumpy building. The downtown campus was on Franklin Street, around the corner from Washington. It was a walk-up with real narrow stairways, one of those real old buildings. The floor by the bursar's office was slanted straight down—it was like being on a slide. It was real dark.

Austin High School was a modern building. By comparison, Austin was beautiful.

So when I saw what a dumpy, rickety building it was, I said I wasn't going to go to school there. I told Vince that. He registered, and I didn't.

Vince called me that night, and he said, "I don't know what to make of you." I said, "Well, I'm not going to go to school in a place that looks like that."

He said, "Well, if you want to go to Loyola University, that's the downtown campus. But Loyola is bigger than that old building. The building doesn't matter." So he convinced me, and the next night I went back and registered. And of course he was right. The building didn't matter.

We used to meet for dinner before classes. There was this restaurant in the telephone building at Washington and Franklin. You could get two pork chops, two lamb chops, or halibut steak, with potatoes and vegetables and a roll and coffee, for sixty-five cents. We were there three nights a week, and whoever got there first ordered. We'd have the pork chops on Monday, the lamb chops on Wednesday, and the halibut on Friday.

Vince would want to pay for my dinner, and I'd say, "No, I'm paying for my own dinner. If I let you pay, later you'll be saying that you paid my way through college."

After school we would walk to the el together, but then we would get on different sides of the platform. By this time Vince was living on the North Side, and my family had moved back east, back to Flournoy Street. I'd say, "What are you living on that dumpy North Side for? Why don't you come down to the great West Side?"

I would get on the Garfield Park el and get off at Independence Boulevard, and he would get on the el for the North Side. This was before they built the subway. He would be on one side of the platform, and I would be on the other. We'd wave to each other. He went north, and I went west.

"You Used to Be a Good Student"

Ma was in bed for months. At first I stayed home from school and did what I could for her. I did everything. I washed her up, fixed her bed, changed her nightgown, fed her breakfast. I worked all the time.

I got up early in the morning and got my father's breakfast—two soft-boiled eggs in a big cup, a couple of pieces of toast, and coffee. Then I made his lunch—two sandwiches, a piece of fruit. Wrapped 'em in newspaper, tied it with a string or a rubber band.

Christmas Day my father made stewed chicken with potatoes. It was nothing like having a turkey. We must have gotten something for Christmas, but I can't remember.

He brought my mother out—carried her out—and put her on the couch in the dining room so she could see the Christmas tree. She was there maybe a half hour or so, and then he carried her back. She was so weak.

This was Arthington Street. About the middle of January we got Mrs. Ahern, who lived two doors down, to stay with Ma, and I went back to school, to Our Lady of Sorrows. But I couldn't leave until after Mrs. Ahern came, and she had her own kids to get off first.

Now wouldn't the sisters know that my mother was sick? The priest used to come every time she got real bad and anoint ma and give her the last rites. But they never said a word to me about that. And I can remember twice when I was embarrassed in class.

One day we came back from lunch. We came in and sat down, and the sister said, "Josephine Ryan, stand up." I stood up. This is eighth grade. She said, "Sister Mary John was in here at lunchtime, and she was looking at the work on the board. She asked me who the third panel belonged to. I told her it was Josephine Ryan. And she said, 'Why, she wrote better than that when she was in my class.' " Sister Mary John was my first-grade teacher. So then I sat down. That was the end of the conversation.

Another time: stand up. So I stood up, and she said, "You know, you used to be a good student. But you're sloping on your oars."

Lunchtime, as soon as I got in the door, Mrs. Ahern ran to her house to get lunch for her kids. I would fix the lunch for Ed and Rosemarie. Marge was in high school. She didn't come home for lunch.

And then I'd always be running back to school. I couldn't go until Mrs. Ahern came back, and she wouldn't come back until maybe she straightened up the dishes or something. Then I would run to school, and sometimes I'd be late. I could have told them my mother . . . I know I never said outright that my mother was sick, but they must have known. I mean, every time she got bad the priest would come. And us four kids would kneel at the foot of the bed, and the priest would be saying the prayers in Latin.

Mock Wedding

My mother and father's twenty-eighth wedding anniversary was April 27, 1938. We went to St. Agatha's in the morning and there was a mass for them. That's where they were married and where the first three of us were baptized. It's at Kedzie Avenue and Douglas Boulevard.

And John and Ann Smith, they loved Ma and Pa, and they came and he sang the mass for them.

Catherine came over and baked a ham. We got them out somehow, going to an afternoon matinee or something. We got a cake and we bought flowers for the table. We really surprised them. We had all sorts of people. It was quite an occasion. And we put on a mock wedding. Marguerite was the groom and big Neil with a lace curtain over his head was the bride and Vince was the preacher. He went to the library and got a book that had some wedding deal in it that he read to them. It was real good.

And Eleanor's husband, Heggie, was walking around with a broomstick during the ceremony, pointing it at the groom. We had a good time. And Ma and Pa enjoyed it. They were surprised for once.

"I Don't Believe in Funerals!"

In 1937, at Sears, I routed the collectors all over the five midwestern states. We had a big map with pins where the accounts were, and then you would decide that the collector would go here, there, and the other place. You'd center the collector around a Sears store and then he could operate from there. You'd send his mail to the store.

They got travel expenses—$1.10 a day for meals and $1.25 a day for hotel. If you wanted to live better you were on your own.

I remember one day a collector came in. He'd been in Paducah, Kentucky, and he said, "Do you know how far Route 1 is from Paducah?"

And I said, "No. How would I know?"

He said, "It's about forty miles straight into the sticks, to collect five dollars?" He said, "How come you don't know? How far have you been from Chicago?"

I said, "Oh, maybe a radius of fifty miles."

He said, "Look, girl, get yourself a ten-dollar ticket down to the Mississippi Delta some weekend, just so you can say you've been somewhere."

And then there was the time I went to mass on Sunday and this guy a few pews up looked like Mr. Perkins. Well, I suddenly realized that Mr. Perkins was going to be in Lincoln, Illinois, on Monday morning and I'd forgotten to send the accounts out. So I panicked, I didn't know what to do.

So I called my boss, Mr. Henderson, and told him that the most awful thing had happened.

And he said, "Oh, that's all right. We'll call the store in the morning and ask them to give him a few of their own accounts and you can get ours out for Tuesday."

But if I hadn't called him he would have raised the roof off the place. He was one of those guys who screamed and yelled.

And whenever you got a raise, which you got maybe once a year, he would call you over and spend about twenty minutes telling you that you got the raise not because you deserved it but out of the kindness of his heart. That's true. And you could never tell anyone what you made. That was company policy. At Sears, salaries were secret.

Then there was Dusty Rhodes. He was a collector we hired in Columbus, Ohio, one December.

Now what we'd do, we'd pick out the overdue accounts and we'd send them to a collector, and on the bottom we'd write COLLECT OR PICK UP, if what the customer owed on was something the collector could pick up.

Anyway, Dusty Rhodes gets the accounts in Columbus and he goes around on Christmas Eve. The people are putting up their Christmas trees and he's hauling the furniture out.

So the day after Christmas we get a call from the Columbus store manager. "Where did you get this guy?"

So Henderson decided the collector should come into the office right away. So Dusty comes in. He was about six foot four, red hair, real terrific looking. But he was going to do the job right.

He said, "That's what you said, so that's what I did. Nobody said anything about you didn't work Christmas Eve."

He was wonderful. He was great. He was still collecting when I left the place.

And then there was this other collector. He was in Quincy, Illinois, and his mother-in-law died, so he came back to Chicago for the funeral. And Henderson had a fit. He said, "I don't believe in funerals!"

And everybody said, "There's one he's going to believe in." And I'm sure he's had it by now, 'cause he was a lot older than I was.

NO LONGER NO
PAYMENT/OKAY TO REFILE

About six months after he left Sears, Chuck Hanna called me up and asked me if I'd come work with him at Spiegel's. He said, "Look, you get $37.50 a week to start." I was making $23. He said, "It won't be long before you're making more than that."

So I went over there to talk to Mr. McDonald. I talked to Chuck first, and he said, "Now, don't give him any business about how you want to advance and that sort of thing. Tell him you want to make money. That's why you'd leave Sears to come here—because they'd pay you for it. He doesn't like any of this guff. And sometimes he talks in circles to see if you're listening. So pay attention. If he says something you don't understand, tell him you don't know what he's talking about."

And that's how it went. So anyway, I got the job. I'd been at Sears ten and a half years. A lot of people thought I was very foolish to leave, because after ten years you got three dollars in profit sharing for every dollar you earned.

This one girl in the accounting division—I went around saying good-bye to people—she said, "You know, I think you're so smart to be leaving, because every year they give you a little more profit sharing—and then you stay because you can't do any better." She said, "Are you really going to make $37.50 a week?"

I said, "Yes."

She said, "How long have you been here?"

I told her, "Ten and a half years."

"How much do you make?"

"Twenty-three dollars a week."

She said, "I've been here twenty years, and I make twenty-two dollars."

Isn't that awful?

But she got the profit sharing later on. I went to a wake one day, and there was a whole row of these women that had been at Sears for years and years. Somebody said, "There's a lot of gold in dem dere hills." And there was. They ended up with a lot of money eventually.

My life would have been so different if I'd stayed at Sears. I might be rich, but I wouldn't have anything else.

I've still got a book that was given to me the day I left. It's dated April 16, 1941, and there's a stamp on the flyleaf, NO LONGER NO PAYMENT/OKAY TO REFILE.

This was a stamp we would put on our cases once they made a payment. Then we would send it off to the regular collection department.

Under the stamp my friend Irv Melamed wrote, "I'm awfully sorry about that."

Seeing Vince Off

Now Tom McLaughlin, he was almost ready to get out of the army when the war came. He'd been drafted years before, with the idea that this war was going on in Europe and we were going to be ready. So then he was in for the duration.

Rosemarie's friend Bill went in December of '41, just after Pearl Harbor. My brother Ed went in July of '42, and then Vince went in August.

I went in to see Chuck Hanna, and I told him that Vince was going into the service the next morning. He said, "Well, go see him off."

So we went to Our Lady of Sorrows for mass in the morning, and then I saw him off downtown at the train station. When I got to work Mr. Hanna called me into his office. "What was it like?"

I said, "It was terrible. Here all these women are, hanging on to these men. And then after the men got on the train, the women are all hanging on to the posts outside the train, and they're all crying and screaming."

He said, "Get the hell out of here. I called you in here to sympathize with you. I see you don't need it."

I said, "All is not lost. He's only going to Camp Grant." I thought it was ridiculous the way they were carrying on in the station, like they would never see them again. It's true, some never did. But they were just going to Rockford—Camp Grant was in Rockford.

Ma had a friend, Mrs. Wells, who lived in Rockford. She said, "Well, why don't you have Jo come up for a weekend? She can stay here and visit Vince at Camp Grant."

I made arrangements to go, and then I got a call. Vince was shipping out. He was going to Texas. He wouldn't be there. So I called Mrs. Wells and told her, "I'm sorry, he shipped out yesterday." She said, "Why don't you bring your sister Rosemarie with you instead? We can have a nice time. We'll show you the town. We have a lot of things we were going to do with you, and we can still do them."

So Rosemarie and I went. We were wined and dined— wonderful meals and all that. But I was never so bored in my life. The thought that I was going to see Vince up there, and now here I am with my sister. I love my sister but . . .

One of the things about that trip that I've always remembered, they had shelves loaded with food—canned food in the basement, all the way to the ceiling. If Mrs. Wells would use a can for dinner, the next day she would go to the store and buy that same exact can to put in the basement. This was because things were being rationed and you needed blue points to get canned goods. They were afraid that the war would go on and on and there would be nothing to eat. They were sure there were going to be shortages. But you should have seen the meals they put on the table. They were gigantic.

That taught me something—don't be so selfish. If the rest of the world is going to starve, starve with them.

Corporal Vincent M. Clark, 1943, Orlando, Florida.

"Don't Come to the Church On Time"

The morning of my wedding, Catherine came over to help me get ready. She started putting my makeup on. I said, "Don't put it on so heavy." She said, "Do you think that I would make you look terrible for your wedding day?"

The flowers came. My mother was a little woman, and she looked at her corsage and said, "I'm not wearing that. It's too big for me." So she took the whole corsage apart, and she made it small and put it on her coat.

Then Frank, the best man, comes running up. He says, "Don't come to the church on time. Vince forgot your cross. He had to go back home to get it."

I had a pearl cross that had belonged to my grandmother. I wore it for my First Communion, and I was planning to wear it for my wedding. Vince had taken it home to fix so it would go on a chain, but he'd forgotten to bring it.

When Vince finally got to the church with the cross, the priest says, "Are you getting married today, son?"

"Well, I think so."

"I haven't any baptismal certificate."

"My aunt was supposed to send it."

"Well, she wrote me a letter and she said she couldn't find what church you were baptized in. But she said she would swear on the Bible that you were baptized, so, taking her word for it, I will marry you."

Vince was in uniform. He was a PFC. Ma's friend Mrs. Carr had a son in the navy. He was a lieutenant, and he was in uniform too. His mother says, "Son, roll that carpet down the aisle." So there he is, practically on his knees in front of this army private, rolling the carpet down the aisle.

When Vince got back to base they made him a corporal. So I told him I got him promoted right away.

God's Will

―――――――――

Tom McLaughlin's sister Mary Ellen was getting married
to Bill and we had a shower for her. She was opening the gifts
and my mother said she'd go put the coffee on. But when she
went past the bedroom where the coats were, the window was
up and the room was a complete wreck. The coats were thrown
all over and all the purses were gone. Now people carry their
purses with them, but back then you put your coat and purse
together.

Somebody at the party said it must have been an inside job,
because how else would anybody know where the purses were?
We called the police, and they came and they said that this was
so common. The crooks come by and see a big group of people
in the living room and they know that the purses must be in the
bedroom.

Mary Ellen died the day after her son was born. Billy. He was
born by cesarean section. She seemed all right and then suddenly

she died. And they didn't want to ask what happened. Tom's mother, Grandma Mac, said, "It must have been God's will. I wouldn't ask." It's just ridiculous. And Rosemarie thought so too. She thought it was terrible that they didn't investigate.

Bill moved in with Grandma Mac, and they raised the baby with the help of Rosemarie and Tom, who lived right upstairs. They took Billy along when they went places with their own kids.

Grandma Mac died when Billy was about ten. Not long after Bill remarried, and they moved to the South Side and they never came back.

There Were Very Few Men Because of the War

Vince was scheduled to have a furlough in March 1943. So I called up the chancery office one day and asked if we could be married at mass during Lent. It used to be you couldn't be married during Lent.

The priest said, "Would you say that again?" So I said it again, and he said, "You know, most people call up here and ask, 'Why do we need mass? Can't we get married without a mass?' You're very unusual."

Then he told me starting the twenty-seventh of March—which was the day we were hoping to be married—they'd changed the rules so that servicemen could be married during Lent.

I went to the rectory of Presentation Church at Springfield and Polk Street to make arrangements. The parish priest said we could have no music and no flowers because of Lent and only two attendants. Well, Vince had belonged to the choir at St.

Catherine's, and we always thought that when we got married we'd have the whole choir.

So the priest walked me to the door. I'm standing there crying like crazy, and I said, "Could I come back inside a minute?"

He said, "What do you want to come in for?"

I said, "Well, I don't want to walk down the street like this and have all the neighbors think that you're bawling me out or something."

So he let me come in. Then he said we could have the wedding march and the recessional but no music during the ceremony.

Some people said it was the first time they ever heard the wedding ceremony, because usually the organ was playing or somebody was singing or something.

We were married on the first Saturday of spring. It was a beautiful day. The weather was always beautiful, no matter what I did. I was twenty-eight. Vince was twenty-four.

I always thought he was much older even though I was born first. He used to say, "Just because we didn't start at the same time doesn't mean we can't cross the bridge together."

My father walked me down the aisle, and I was a nervous wreck. I couldn't wait for the music to start. My biggest fear was that the woman who sang the daily mass would start singing. She had one of those gravelly voices, and you never knew what she was singing.

So it was very nice. A lot of people were there. But there were very few men because of the war.

Wedding Night

—◯∕◯—

After our wedding, Ma said, "Was everything the way you wanted it?" I said, "Oh, yes, except nobody threw any rice."

After church, we had a dinner for twenty-five. Loretta Derrick and her mother came over and made chicken, which they put in these little baskets they bought at a bakery. They were part of the meal. Little things, and you put the chicken in the middle with cream sauce, and I remember there were slices of Jell-O with fruit.

My mother borrowed ration stamps from everybody she knew. Blue stamps were for anything in a can. Red stamps were for meat. She had the cake baked at a bakery but they only had tops with a regular bride and groom, which we weren't. So she ran around town to find one with a groom in an army uniform.

The priest said we shouldn't have any liquor, just one glass of wine each, because it was Lent. But we forgot to invite the priest to dinner. Aunt May asked, "When is the priest coming?" We

Wedding day, March 27, 1943,
Mr. and Mrs. Vincent M. Clark.

said, "We don't know." We were afraid to tell her the truth. We did everything the way he wanted it done. But we forgot to invite him.

We had a party that evening. There were about fifty people in our house. The same twenty-five from after church, plus twenty-five extra.

My father said it was one of the most embarrassing moments of his life. He couldn't offer his gentlemen friends another glass of wine or beer because there wasn't any left. You weren't supposed to be celebrating during Lent.

So the plan was to cut the cake, and then we'd go downstairs to Mrs. Trier's, where I could change my clothes for traveling, and then Frank would take us to the train station. So we cut the cake, waved good-bye, and as we started down the hall, we were pelted with rice. I think Ma must have given everybody bags of it. But anyway, she said every time she swept or used the vacuum for years, she picked up rice. There was no end to it.

Taking Mr. Maloney's Job

At Spiegel's I worked in the legal department under Mr. Maloney, who was an attorney. He was a book man.

I remember on my way up in the morning I used to stop on the second floor and pick up some of our accounts and bring them up. And he would start yelling at me that I was late. And I would say, "I'm not late. I've been in the building. I went to get these accounts so we'd have something to work on." He was pretty inefficient.

One day during the war, Mr. McDonald called me in and he said, "We'd like to give you Mr. Maloney's job. Do you know what he does?"

And I said, "Oh, I know how to do it better than he does. Where's he going?"

"He's being fired."

"Wait a minute, I'm not taking that man's job away from him."

"Well, if you don't want it somebody else will. He's not staying. We're letting him go and that's for sure."

So anyway, they fired him and gave me the job.

So I worked with this girl named Anne Doyle, and she said to me, "Vince is coming home for Christmas."

And I said, "No, he's not."

And she said, "Yes, he is."

I said, "How do you know that?"

And she said, "Well, I go to mass in the morning and every morning I pray that he will come home for Christmas."

And on the fifteenth of December he called me and told me that he'd been transferred downstate to Chanute Air Base. He was an instructor on Link trainers, a simulated airplane that they used to train pilots. And he didn't know whether he would get a break for Christmas, but if not I could come down and visit him.

And he did come home for Christmas. He got a three-day pass.

Then every Tuesday he had a day off and he came in and I got the day off with pay. He would come in on Monday night and I would meet him at the IC station and then he would stay at our house and then we'd do something on Tuesday.

I didn't know anybody else at Spiegel's who had someone that near. Most people were at bases farther away or overseas.

All the girls in the office used to meet. Nobody had anyone. They were all gone, their husbands or their boyfriends or whatever it was. So on Wednesday we would go to someone's home after work and have some kind of lunch, not anything fancy. Maybe a sandwich or something. And we would do crocheting, embroidery work. I was trying to learn how to embroider.

The job was good. We handled all the bankruptcy cases.

There were only four of us doing it and I was in charge. But it got so I didn't need to be in charge. We each had our own accounts and did our own thing.

When I left there Mr. McDonald asked me, "Who should I put in charge?" And I said, "Well, to tell you the truth, I was never really in charge. We just all worked together."

"Well, maybe I'll just leave it that way," he said. "People around here have asked me, 'What does she do over there?' "

I was always taking my day off.

May of '43

—————
⚯

In May of '43 Vince was transferred from downstate to an air base in Orlando, Florida. He was to teach celestial navigation, so fliers would be able to navigate by the stars.

He called me and said he was going, and I went into Mr. Hanna's office and told him Vince was shipping out so I'm going to meet him, and I asked to borrow five bucks. He hands me the money and I go. I couldn't have done that at Sears.

I met him in Kankakee. I took the IC, and he said he would meet me at the station. And when I got off he was nowhere to be found. So I went to the cashier and asked if there was anyone around looking for me and he said, "No." But he said, "You know, there's another Kankakee station and he might be at the other station." And just then, I see Vince walking up the path. He had been at the other station.

Then we got on a bus and we went to Rantoul, where Chanute Air Base was. So we had a great day together and he introduced me to all of his friends. And they were all so happy that they were going to Florida instead of to Europe or some other such place.

We went to the PX and we had supper and then he walked me over to the bus and I took the bus home. And I remember it was real late when I got downtown and I took a cab home from there.

Now, some people think it's just recently that people are afraid to be out on the street. But I think it's always been that way, more or less, at night if you were alone. If you had somebody with you, you always felt better. And if you were with a man it was no problem.

Culture Shock

~

In June of '43 I went down to Florida, and we spent three weeks together. I came down on the train and changed at Jacksonville to get the train for Orlando. And I was carrying three cases. There were no redcaps, and I'm struggling. They say, "The train is on the other track. You have to go over there." So I pass this whole crowd of people. But I was so busy holding my luggage that I didn't even look. I got on the train, went to Orlando, but when I got there, Vince wasn't there.

So I waited in the train station. Pretty soon somebody's shouting, there's a telegram for Mrs. Vincent Clark. It says, "Will meet you at the station at three." This is about noon.

The station was real culture shock to me. Because I never saw WHITE ONLY signs for washrooms before. A little black lady with a little cap on her head and an apron came over and asked me if she could get me a cup of tea or coffee. She was from the restaurant across the street. So she brought me a cup of tea. Then I took my telegram out again. And I looked up at the top and I saw Jacksonville, Florida. And then I knew right away what had happened. He'd gone to Jacksonville to meet me. And the guy was pushing us on the train.

He was with a group of people trying to get through and there were MPs standing in the front, and they yelled, "Nobody's getting through till these people get through to the train."

And he's yelling, "My wife's going on that train." But he couldn't get through. He must have been so frustrated. I felt terrible.

So at three o'clock in the afternoon, when the next train came in, he was on it.

This was another culture shock. We found that there was a house with rooms to rent. We went there and the lady came to the door in her bare feet. That to me was, my God, you're walking around the house in your bare feet and you come to the door when the doorbell rings?

But we got a beautiful room there. And then we decided, we had three weeks, so we made a little tour. When we got to Palm Beach we got a room right on the beach, for like three dollars a day, the serviceman's rate. There was a pier right in front of the hotel, out to the water. We rented bikes there and we rode around. I remember seeing the Kennedy compound. That was kind of big stuff.

And then we thought, well, we could go to Miami. But we have it so good here. Why would we leave this? We can always go to Miami some other time. I never did get to Miami.

Three-Month Leave

In October of '43 Vince wrote from Florida and said he had permission to live off base, so I could come down. Well, I knew it would be easier to get away from the family if I said I was taking a three-month leave instead of saying I was quitting my job and going down there for the duration.

All the servicemen were in for the duration of the war, whether they signed up for two years or three years or four years. They were in until it ended.

I went to my immediate supervisor, Miss Henny—we used to call each other Miss and Mrs. in those days. I told her I wanted a three-month leave and would she please tell Mr. McDonald, who was the big boss.

So Mr. McDonald comes over to my desk and says, "I understand you're pregnant." I said, "I'm what?" He said, "Well, Miss Henny told me that you're pregnant and you want a leave." He pulls out the wastebasket and turns it over and sits down on it. And he spends about an hour or more telling me that what my husband wants is for me to stay on that job. Make that money. Put it in the bank. Have something for us to start on when he gets out.

I said, "I think what my husband wants is for me to come down to Florida and live with him." When I got home that night I was boiling mad that she had told him I was pregnant. Then I got a letter from Vince which said, "I'm sorry I built you up like this, but now they tell us we can't live off the base." He was a sergeant by then, but you had to be a staff sergeant to live off base. So I didn't move down until March of '44.

But you know, I was so happy—'cause I could go back to work the next morning and tell Miss Henny, "I'm not going any-where."

The War on Insects

I moved down to Orlando in March of '44, and in July we came home on furlough. We took the bus to Titusville, Florida, to get the train. I was wearing a white suit, white gloves, white purse. We put our bags in a locker at the train station and went into a drugstore. The whole ceiling was black with mosquitoes— the whole place was swarming with them. Well, we went out of there and tried to find a place where we could get away from the mosquitoes, but we couldn't find anyplace.

So we walked back toward the train station, and we passed a bar. The door was wide open, and there was nobody there but the bartender, who was sitting behind the bar. He had a big fan blowing toward the bar, and it was blowing all the mosquitoes away.

We went in and sat down and ordered two drinks, and then when we heard the train coming we ran like crazy to get our bags and get on the train. But when we got on the train there were no seats. The sailors and everybody were sitting in the aisles. Somebody got up and gave me a seat. Vince sat on the floor.

The windows were open, and all these cinders were blowing in. It was the most miserable thing. And when I looked at myself, I had blood all over from swatting the mosquitoes.

Another time we were in Daytona Beach. There were no lights during the war but we went out in the dark for a walk. When we got back to the hotel it was full of sailors and soldiers. We went up to our room and palmetto bugs were flying all over. Vince went down to the desk and asked for another room and the clerk said, "We don't have another room. You can sleep in the hall. That's where the sailors are sleeping tonight." He said, "Here. Here's a squirt can; go up and fight 'em yourself."

So the last I remember, I'm under the sheet and Vince is standing on a chair with the squirt can in his hand. When we woke up in the morning there were dead bugs all over the floor. Did we get out of there in a hurry. Daytona Beach.

"These People Have Ceased"

～

In Orlando I got a job at the ration board. One day an old lady came in because her ration book was all torn up. She would send the kids on the block to the store for her, and she'd tear out the coupons to give to them, and the book was all messed up.

Virginia, who worked with me, was very young. She'd come from Tennessee, or someplace like that, to get a divorce, which was easier in Florida. She was berating this woman about her torn-up ration book. So I went over, and I said, "Virginia, I'll handle this."

I asked the woman to come inside and sit down at my desk, which she did. She had no children. Her husband was gone. She was living alone. So I made her out a new ration book. I put a hard cover on it, and I wrote her name on it, Mary B. Farren. And I told her that when she sent the children to the store, give them the whole book, and the grocer would tear out what was necessary.

As she was leaving she said, "I hope you will never be alone in the world."

Then one day, not too many months after that, a woman who worked at one of the local nursing homes came in. She threw a flock of ration books on the counter, and she said, "These people have ceased." And there was my book from Mary B. Farren.

In August the War Ended

⤏⤎

V-E Day was May 8th, Victory Europe. Then in August the war ended. The fourteenth was V-J Day, Victory Japan. Maude was born a week later. I was in the hospital listening to the radio and I heard the signing of the peace on the battleship *Missouri*. I stayed ten days after she was born. That was how they did it back then. You went home on the eleventh day. While I was waiting to go home, the peace was signed.

Vince was discharged in November. And we were planning to stay in Orlando for the winter and he would get a job on a laundry truck—he knew where he could get one—then we'd go home in the spring. We thought it would be good for the baby, the good weather.

But the house we were living in was sold, so we had to get out. We found a house to buy down there, forty-five hundred dollars. It was a five-room cottage on the back of a lot, with a full lot in front. We had enough for the down payment but it

Ed, Josephine (Mary Jo), Marge, and Rosemarie Ryan,
Chicago Eucharistic Congress, Soldier Field, June 1926.

didn't make any sense if we were going back to Chicago. Our older friends talked us out of it.

So we moved back to the West Side.

Of course the whole family was crazy about Maudemarie, the first baby in the family, the first grandchild. Half the family was at Union Station to meet us. And they brought a warm baby bunting to put the baby in. We were sure they came to see the baby, not us. My parents were there, and Rosemarie and Marge, and Ed, who had just come home from Europe the week before.

It was the fifteenth of December, 1945. Saturday. And it was eighty-five degrees when we left Florida and it was ten below zero when we got to Chicago.

Second Grade: "I've Never Forgotten Your Face"

One day, not too many years ago, I was at work and this man comes in. He walks right past the sign that says Authorized Personnel Only, and he walks straight over to my desk in the middle of the office and says, "Were you in second grade at the Ericson School?" I hadn't been at this job very long, and my supervisor was not a very considerate woman, so I was a little uncomfortable having him there. I said, "Well, yes, I went to Ericson. It was the only year I ever went to a public school, when I was in second grade."

He said, "That's where I know you from. I've never forgotten your face. You look just the same." He told me his family had been the first Italian family in the neighborhood. Then he said, "Why, that was more than fifty years ago!"

I said, "Hey, wait a minute. Not so loud. The people here don't know I'm that old."

He said, "Well, I'm glad I saw you again." And he left.

After he was gone I felt so terrible that I hadn't asked him any questions. If I'd been friendly to him I would have learned something.

I couldn't for the life of me figure out why he remembered me. I went back in my mind to second grade, to 1921, 1922. What happened? The reason we went to Ericson was because there was no kindergarten at Our Lady of Sorrows for my brother Ed. My mother and father did a lot of arguing—my father wanted us all to go to the public school so we could take Ed with us.

Ericson was only a block away, down to Harrison Street and around the corner, and that way we could take care of Ed. My mother would say, "No, they have to go to the Catholic school."

So my father promised her that if we went to the public school this one year, next year we would go back to Our Lady of Sorrows. Which is what we did.

Now, the reason they wanted us all to go to school together, rather than letting Ed stay home, was because my mother was expecting a baby. The baby was born on a Saturday night in the room next to us. We were asleep. We didn't know what was going on.

Sunday morning we woke up, and we had this beautiful baby brother, James. So we went to nine o'clock mass, and when we came home we brought all the kids on the block in to see him.

Two days later, on Tuesday morning, James was lying on the dining-room table in his christening clothes with a handkerchief over his face. He had died during the night.

The undertaker came and put the baby in this little white casket. My mother was in bed. In those days you were supposed to stay in bed for ten days after childbirth. My father carried the casket in so my mother could say good-bye.

Then Marge and I went with my Aunt Anna and my father to Calvary Cemetery, where my mother's mother is buried and my older brother and sister, John and Loretta, who also died young. They were born naturally, and then died a week or so later. They're all buried at Calvary, the first two children and then the seventh. My mother always reminded us of their birthdays. She would say, "We have three angels in heaven praying for us."

For weeks and weeks I kept thinking back to the year James was born, to second grade at Ericson School, to try and remember this man who'd come into my office.

Marge and Ed and I would all walk to school together. At Sacramento and Harrison there was always a policeman to help us cross the street, and then one day they installed the new stop-and-go lights. The policeman explained how the lights worked, and he said, "Now you don't need me anymore. You can cross the street on your own." We were very sorry to see him go.

That was the year we used to get penny ice cream cones in the store next to the school. We went to a fair downtown at Christmastime. And we had a gym on the top floor of the school. I never had another gym in my life until I got to high school.

That was the year Marge lost Rosemarie's ring.

We used to go to the show that year. On payday my father would take us to the Harrison Theater on Kedzie, right where the Eisenhower Expressway is now. It would be twenty cents for an adult and ten cents for children, so for eighty cents the whole family went to the show. And for twenty cents he bought four packages of Cracker Jacks, a nickel each.

We would go on Thursday night, which was amateur night, and this one night some kids from my class were doing a Japanese dance that we'd learned in gym class. They were singing and twirling umbrellas. I knew all the girls on stage.

Anyway, as hard as I tried, I couldn't place this man in my mind. He was small and dark, with curly black and gray hair. He didn't tell me his name. Just that he was the first Italian in the neighborhood.

Then one day I remembered something else. Each day there would be a boy of the day and a girl of the day. Everyone got a turn choosing. It was my turn to choose the boy of the day, and I chose Tony. The teacher called him up in front of the room and said, "Tony, did you wash your face today?"

He said, "No."

"Tony, did you comb your hair today?"

He said, "No."

Then she turned to me and said, "Josephine, how can you choose a boy for the day who has neither washed his face nor combed his hair? Virginia, you choose the boy of the day."

So I think that must have been Tony that day in my office so many years later. And that's why he remembered me.

No Afternoon Nap

All the years at Sears I was happy enough. But when I left I was on cloud nine.

At Spiegel's I was a junior executive. The first Christmas I got a bonus of $125. That was the first bonus I ever got. No—I got $50 from Sears for their fiftieth anniversary. Anyway, the $125 bonus was just the greatest thing. And then after I was at Spiegel's for about a year I made $50 a week. I'd been making $23 at Sears.

I worked in a collection laboratory. We composed letters, and then we tested them to see what the results were. If the result was good, then we passed it on to the collection department. They would use it as a form letter.

We had letters that said, "You are vulnerable. You have not paid us. You will pay. The amount is so much." A lot of trick words, trick letters. I used some of that stuff when I went to Alden's twenty-some years later. They thought it was terrific.

Now, when I went to Spiegel's I thought Mr. Hanna was going to be my boss. That was a disappointment. It turned out that Mr. Schumacher was my boss. Chuck was over the whole area, but I worked directly for Schumacher, Bill Schumacher. He's now a priest in Dallas, Texas.

But when I first went to Spiegel's I wasn't very happy. For one thing, at Sears I would take a ten-minute nap every afternoon in the lounge at two o'clock. They had a beautiful lounge with big couches. But when I went to Spiegel's there was no lounge. All there was was a washroom with a hard chair in it.

And every day at two o'clock I could not stay awake. I would go in the washroom and sit there on this hard chair and try to get a few winks so I could wake up. People would come in and say, "What are you doing? Don't you feel well?" I was so used to my two o'clock nap.

Maudemarie

It was a Sunday. We called a cab and we were riding to the hospital. I said to Vince, "Wouldn't it be a beautiful day to go on a picnic?" And the driver turned around and looked at me like I was out of my mind.

She was born in two and a half hours. In those days the father didn't go into the delivery room. But afterwards they let him come in to see me. He looked so worried that I said, "Vince, don't worry about me. They're being wonderful to me. Everything's fine."

He wanted to name the baby Peggy, Margaret Mary, after his mother. And I wanted it to be Maudemarie, after my mother. I said, "My mother is alive and she would enjoy having a child named for her." And we could name our second daughter for his mother. And he said, "Well, why don't we settle it by making it Mary Jo." And I said, "Oh, no." We could keep that one for later too.

When she was born the doctor said to me, "I never saw such wide-awake eyes. What's her name?"

I said, "I don't know."

He said, "What's your name?" I think he wanted to see if I was awake. I said, "Mary Jo."

So I slept for a while. In those days they took the baby to the nursery.

Anyway, when Vince came in to see me, he said, "We have a beautiful baby girl. Do you know what her name is?"

I said, "No, I don't."

He said, "It's Maudemarie." She's always liked her name and I told her that her father named her. That I didn't.

If we'd had a boy it would have been Vincent or John Ryan.

We had five names when the first one was born. So we didn't have to worry about names for years. We used them all eventually.

The Witch She Was

While I was away in Orlando, my parents moved back to Austin, to Monroe Street out near Cicero Avenue. And the first thing my mother told me was, "We don't wrap our garbage in newspaper now. We have to put it in a brown paper bag." This was to show me how good the new neighborhood was.

Ma's friend Mrs. Carroll found the apartment for her. She knew the landlady, Mrs. O., and she knew what a problem she was. But she thought my mother could get along with anybody.

Mrs. O.'s husband had died tragically. He hung himself in the basement. And Mrs. Carroll knew this, but she didn't tell my mother because she thought it would be a little too scary.

After it happened, the neighbors came in to help out and then they walked around saying that she had a dirty house. And that closed her off from the neighbors. She would have nothing to do with anybody. And that's how she became the witch she was. Her only friend was Mrs. G., who lived next door.

And she liked my mother. Ma took her different places, to the women's club and stuff like that.

It was a six-room apartment. So when we came back from Orlando, we moved in with my parents. Housing was very difficult to find after the war. And my parents needed support. I'd always sent them half of what I earned. When I got the job at the ration board, it was government so you weren't paid very promptly in the beginning. And my mother was worried stiff. Somebody told her it must be volunteer work. Vince said, "If your mother's so worried, why don't you go to the bank and draw out two weeks or whatever and send it to her?" Which I did. And then eventually my paychecks came through. I was making like thirty dollars a week and I'd send her fifteen.

The apartment had three bedrooms. We had one bedroom with the baby, and my mother and father had a bedroom, and Vince used the third bedroom as a study. It was off the living room. And he kept his clothes in the closet up there. And so that's where he dressed and studied.

The windows in the dining room looked out onto the yard and the alley. And after the kids came you'd see Mrs. O. go out the back door and she'd walk around the block and come in the front and almost dare you to make any noise, because you would not think she was there. And then, once she heard noise, she pounded on the pipes, on the radiators. And whenever the kids had a day off from school, that was the day she made sure to pound on the pipes for something.

One Sunday Vince was reading the comics to the kids and the doorbell rang and he went to the door and there was Mrs. O. She said, "What are those kids doing up there?"

He said, "They're sitting on little red chairs and their father was reading the Sunday comics to them." She says, "I don't know why I should have all your damn kids in my house." And he said, "We only have four now. But we may have ten." And of course she slammed the door on him.

She got worse after my father died but she was still halfway decent until my mother died. Then she went all out.

It was very difficult to find an apartment. And if you did find one they didn't want kids. So then we went looking for houses but we didn't have enough for a down payment. So we stayed on, until Vince got out of law school. Anyway, we had been there eight years when we found the house on Menard.

We had been packing boxes for weeks. You were four. We'd send you over to the National on the corner and you'd come home with a cardboard box. You loved doing it and every now and then you were able to buy a nickel candy bar. We had the living room practically filled with boxes all ready to go.

B.J. and Vince both worked for an insurance company, and they had two company cars, exactly alike, and they went out and rented two identical red trailers.

Neil got everything organized upstairs, and he'd send the guys down with the stuff to put in the first trailer and then off it would go, and then a little while later the second car would pull up and they would start loading that trailer.

I stayed at the apartment, Rosemarie was at the new house. We moved everything except the big things—the piano, the refrigerator, the stove. The movers were coming the next day.

All the kids had been farmed out. Kevin was a baby so we took him with us and we stayed in the new house, the old new house.

The Smiths had left so many things for us. It was a nine-room house and we were coming from a six-room apartment. Would we like the trunks full of World War I uniforms? They left books and bookcases up in the attic. A breakfront. Old *Esquire* maga-zines. A settee.

They left the bed that's still in my bedroom today, with three brand-new-looking mattresses on top. We brought a playpen for Kevin and that's where we stayed that night. We slept on top of those three mattresses.

The next morning I got up and looked out the window and saw the big backyard, with peonies from the back door all the way around to the back fence, and I got hysterical because on Monroe Street there was one flower in the middle of the yard with a fence around it and then there was another fence around the whole yard, and the kids weren't allowed to even step in it. They always played in the alley, or one door over in the court-yard of the apartment building.

Vince said, "Calm down. You can spend your whole life look-ing out at the yard."

So then we went back and started cleaning the apartment. We did every window. We scrubbed all the floors and the wood-work, cleaned the bathroom, the cabinets, everything. There was nothing left except a bar of soap and a roll of toilet paper. Everything else was out.

Vince went with the movers and I stayed at the apartment. I was down on my hands and knees scrubbing the floor, and I have the baby in my arm and I'm nursing him. My brother Ed walks in and says, "What in the hell do you think you're doing?" I said, "I'm scrubbing the floor." He said, "No you're not. You're nursing a baby. Go nurse the baby. I'll scrub the floor."

Vince came back and then, as we were about to leave, our in-surance man, Jimmy Fitzgerald, came to see about the insurance for the new house. He walked through the place and he said, "I have never been in an apartment that looked this clean. Anybody could move right in. You sure must have had some good bringing up about you." And he was right. That was my father's rule: always leave the house better than when you came.

So Jimmy left and then Vince and I and the baby went downstairs to say goodbye to Mrs. O. And she came to the door and Vince gave her so much money for the days we had stayed over. It was the second or third of June. He said, we had the plumber in to clean the drains. Here's the paid bill for that. And then he gave her some money because the movers had broken a pane of glass in the built-in dish cabinet.

She took everything and then she said, "And good luck to you, Mary." And we walked out. I swear, it was the happiest day in my life.

A few days later I called up the neighbor next door to give her our new address and she said that after we left Mrs. O. called Mrs. G. to take her up so she could see what a mess we had made of the place, and Mrs. G. told her, "I know all about apartments, I have looked at many. But I have never seen a cleaner, more perfect apartment in my whole life."

So we got the last laugh.

Rosemarie and Tom

Apartments were hard to find after the war. When Rosemarie and Tom McLaughlin got married in May of '46, all they could find was a furnished place. It had a living room and a bedroom. The bath was down the hall. Everybody shared the kitchen and the bath. The building was on Jackson, on the corner of Spaulding or Homan. It was a white stone building, real old.

But Rosemarie was happy they didn't have to move in with us, or with her mother-in-law. They didn't find the apartment until a week before the wedding.

They went to Niagara Falls on their honeymoon. Tom didn't want to go. He didn't like to fly. But you know Rosemarie. She wanted to go so they went. They flew and they got back all right.

I got a call from Mrs. McLaughlin one day. She said, "I understand Rosemarie's going over there today. I want you to tell her that the apartment upstairs from me is for rent. The people just moved out." I was startled but I said, "Okay, I'll tell her." I got off the phone and I told my mother and we both laughed and laughed. I said there was no way that Rosemarie would want to live over her mother-in-law. But when I told her, she said, "That's wonderful." We were both flabbergasted. She said, "We can buy furniture. We can start having a home."

So they moved in above her mother-in-law. The building was on the North Side on Cicero Avenue. They were above a tavern. And she had no trouble at all with Mrs. McLaughlin. She used to tell her husband in the morning, "Good-bye, have a good day, now drop in and see your mother." So he'd drop in and have a cup of coffee with his mother on his way to work. Then he'd go out and get on the Cicero Avenue bus.

Anyway, they lived there for quite a long time. Tom, Pat and Mike were all born while they were there. The apartment in the front became available. The people were moving out. Now that was like six rooms. They only had four in back. So the kids could have their own bedroom. And there was a nice living room with big windows looking out on Cicero Avenue. They were right above the tavern. She always figured, in the daytime nobody was there. So the kids could make all the noise they wanted. And of course she looked at us and saw what it was like when you had to always think about the landlady downstairs.

Now of course Tom painted and decorated the new place. And then they were there for years and years and years. She liked living above the tavern, and watching the traffic on Cicero. She always said, "If you're going to live in the city, you might as well be in the city."

I don't remember why they moved off Cicero. But they moved a couple of blocks west on Altgeld. They were gonna get civilized now. The kids were grown a bit. They were on the first floor and Tom painted the new place and they decorated the basement too. We used to have parties down there. Anyway, the landlady was a witch. So after a year or two they moved back to Cicero Avenue, just up the street from their old place. It was above a rug store, or something quiet like that. There was never anybody down there in the evening. So she didn't have to worry about the kids making noise or having their friends up. So Tom painted and decorated the new apartment. And then suddenly, the people who were next door to them decided to move out. It was a bigger, corner apartment, with south windows and the sun coming in. So Rosemarie decided she wanted to move there. Well, that's when she said they almost got a divorce. He'd just finished painting six rooms, and then this place was seven rooms. He said to me, "How many times must I go through this?" But he did it. I think she called up a lot of people to come help him paint.

When I bought this building I asked Rosemarie if she and Tom would ride through the neighborhood and tell me what she thought of it. I said, "I know the inside is nice enough, but what do you think of the outside? It's a small lot. It's near Irving Park."

So they rode around. And then she called me up. And she said, "If you're going to live in the city, you might as well be in the city. Irving Park is a good street. And it looks like it's a real nice place."

Where did they go from Cicero Avenue?

They moved to Sunnyside, to the first floor of a three-flat. Tom and Rosemarie did all the gardening. They planted flowers at their own expense. They took care of the whole place. They shoveled the snow, they cut the grass. And they were never paid anything, and they never asked for anything. So anyway, the landlord comes around one year and tells them that she's raising the rent like twenty-five dollars a month. It was a real lot. People only raised the rent by five or ten dollars in those days.

Rosemarie said to the landlord, "How about all the money we've spent over the years on flowers and grass seed, and our labor? We've never been paid anything for it." And the woman said, "Well, that has nothing to do with the taxes. The taxes have gone up. So I have to raise your rent."

So they were mad, and they came over here. Tom said, "How would you like us for tenants upstairs?" And I said, "You mean it?" He said, "Of course I mean it." And I said, "I think that would be very nice."

Tom was already sick. He had been to the doctors and he knew he had cancer. They'd already scheduled the operation. And I was happy we were going to have a man in the building. Anyway, the building flooded in the spring, and Rosemarie and I went down to the basement to try and save what we could. Tom had hardly been out of bed for weeks. But he got up and came running down the steps to tell us not to touch any electrical appliances.

When he died and Rosemarie came home from the hospital, she said, "Now we know why he wanted to move here."

House for Rent

We were living on Monroe Street, with six children and with a landlady downstairs who didn't like us very much. So we were always looking for a house to buy, but we never had enough for the down payment. And nobody'd rent to us. We'd find places for rent but nobody'd rent to you with six kids.

I remember one day we were going out to Oak Forest to look at a house. We were at about 146th and Halsted and I said, "How much further?" And Vince says, "Oh, it's a way yet." I said, "Well, you better turn around. This is too far already."

Another time we went out to Hinsdale to see a place for fifteen hundred down. It was up on a hill. It was five rooms if you pulled a divider between a room and made two bedrooms out of it. My mother was going to be with us. It had a little sun room off the living room. And we could make that a bedroom for her, and it had a door you could close. It was just a little place but at least she'd have her own room. And then the kids could have the two bedrooms with the divider. And then there was one other bedroom.

There was a pond down at the bottom of this big hill in front of the house. As soon as I saw the pond, I thought of my kids and that was as far as I'd go. Vince was sort of for it because it was only fifteen hundred down, and we had that much. But he didn't like the pond either. Anyway, so we decided that was not it.

One day I see an ad in the paper. A six-room house for rent, basement, attic. So I call up. And I said, "Well, I have six children." And this guy says, "That's okay."

He told me the house was only a few years old. He owned it with his sister. But his sister had gotten married and moved away, and what was a single guy going to do with a big house like this? So he decided to rent it. The house was in Wheaton. He told me the address. But he said, "Don't go out to see it before Friday, because we're doing some cleaning and stuff."

I can't remember what the rent was, but it wasn't a lot. We were paying seventy-five a month where we were.

He didn't ask for a deposit but I thought, if you want to make something solid you better give him one. So I said, "Would you accept a deposit?" And he said, "Yes, if you want to give me one."

Well, when Vince left to go to work that morning, I told him this guy was coming over and I'd need some money to give him. He said, "Well, OK, I'll put something on the mantel. You can give him that. But make sure he's not a crook." And I said, "Oh, there's no problem there. I'll know if he's a crook."

So the man came and he sat down and told me some more about the house. I remember he said when you push the doorbell chimes ring in the house. And of course I was just thrilled at this idea that we'd be getting out of this apartment.

I go over to the mantel and I see five ten-dollar bills. And I think, well, he didn't ask me for a deposit, so I'll just give him ten dollars. So I took one ten and gave it to him and he wrote a receipt.

Then I said, "Come on in the bedroom and meet my mother. She'll be moving there with us."

My mother was in bed; this was after her stroke. She couldn't talk, just be-be-be-be-be. So I introduced them and told her about the house.

Well, he looked like he was ready to run out of there. He said, "Well, I'll be seeing you. I know you'll like the house." And he hurried out of the bedroom, opened the door, and went down the stairs. And I went back in and my mother went, "Be-be-be-be-be."

I said, "What's wrong? You don't believe it?" And she went, "Be-be-be-be-be-be-be."

"You mean he's a crook?"

And she nodded her head and said, "Be-be-be."

She knew exactly what she wanted to say. She was very clear in the head. She really was. To the very last she always knew. And I could talk to her. In fact, sometimes I think of conversations we had, and I know she couldn't talk. But we talked.

Well, anyway. Two nights later we went to a church meeting. And we told all our friends that we were going to get this house. They were sad that we were going to move away but they were very happy for us.

My sister Marge was baby-sitting for us. So when we came home, she says, "Oh, you had a call from the police station." They wanted us to call when we came in. So Vince calls and they say, "We have a man here who's been renting a house in Wheaton. He was at your house and you gave him a ten-dollar deposit."

Winter 1947–48. Vince is holding Vincent, and Mary Jo is holding Maudemarie.

Vince said, "Yeah?"

"Well, he's rented it to twenty other people too."

I guess what happened, one of the people he rented to decided to drive out and see the house. They didn't care if they saw the inside. They just wanted to see this beautiful house, that they'd put a down payment on. So they drove out. They had the address, the exact address he'd given them. But when they got out there it was an institution of some kind, a school or something.

See, what he'd done, he'd rented a room in a rooming house, got a phone, and put an ad in the paper. And the police caught him in bed.

Vince thought I was pretty sharp, that I'd only given him ten dollars. A lot of people had given him much more.

Mary, the Real Estate Lady

One day I saw an ad for a house near Columbus Park. It was on two lot, it had gas heat, two bathrooms, and I can't remember what else. All the things we couldn't afford. Anyway, it was very attractive. I called the real estate office and a woman answered. I said, "I saw your ad in the paper." And she said, "Oh, I thought you were Catherine from the Austin Bank." And I said, "No. But that's what I need, money."

Anyway, when she told me the price, I asked if these people would sell it on contract. I had just recently learned about that. She said, "No. But wait just a minute. Would you mind a house that doesn't have a downstairs bathroom? It only has one upstairs." I said, "I don't care where the bathroom is, as long as there's a roof on it. I've got six children and I've been looking for a house for a while."

She told me the house was two doors from Columbus Park. The people were anxious to sell but most people wanted a bathroom downstairs. This place also had a coal furnace. And everybody wanted gas or oil. She said, "These people like to show the house on Thursday afternoon. Because that's the day they bake bread. Could you see it then?" I said of course. And then she gave me the address and it was on Menard, right down the street from where we'd lived in 1939 and '40.

It was a big old house. I loved it the minute I saw it. Kevin was two or three months old. This was March 1954. And the house smelled wonderful from the baking bread. But I could not remember ever seeing it before, although I knew I must have passed it every day on my way to and from Sears. But we hadn't been there in fifteen years.

The Smiths lived there. The three Smith girls. They were in their sixties and seventies. They had lived in the house since 1908. Forty-six years. There'd been thirteen children. And one brother died. He was helping to pave the front walk with his father, and it was real bad weather and he got pneumonia, I think that's what it was.

Anyway, the stairway leading up to the second floor was just beautiful. And I thought, oh, to have a house with a stairway like that.

These three women, they just loved Kevin to pieces. They put him on a couch in the middle room, and two of them stayed with him while Mary Smith walked around with us.

We took a quick look at the living room. And then she took us through the big dining room and the little kitchen. She was going to show us the basement next. Well, as we went down the steps, I looked out at the big backyard. And the real estate agent was right alongside of me and I said, "This is beautiful." And she said, "Mrs. Clark, don't say it too loud. If people think you really like it, they're not going to come down on the price." But I couldn't contain myself.

So we looked at the basement, which wasn't much to look at. It was unfinished. There was a coal furnace, which took up a big part of the basement, and a toilet, no sink. There were a couple of washtubs. So then we went upstairs to the second floor. And there were five bedrooms. Well, we started at the front. They were very nice rooms. Big, double exposures. And then we got to the main bedroom. It had a fireplace and a big bay window, three windows looking out toward Columbus Park.

And then we went to the back two rooms. One of the rooms had a window facing east, but the window was on a stairway, and then there was another window on the other side of the stairway looking out the back of the house. Well, to find out that the house had a back stairway all the way to the basement, that was great.

Then we went up to the attic, which had so many things in it, old furniture and trunks. You could have spent a day there, just looking. It was unfinished. But it had one skylight near the back, and it had windows on the front and the sides. I looked out the front windows and I remembered that when we lived down the block there used to be an old, tumbledown-looking house down this way. It was painted a dark color, and it had dirty curtains in the windows. We knew that an old man lived there all by himself.

One night, on my way home from Sears, I walked past the house and down the block and into the kitchen where my mother was cooking dinner. And I said, "You know, Ma, I just had the greatest idea. I was walking by that old house down the block, and I was thinking, wouldn't it be great if I fell on the sidewalk someday and that old man came out and said, 'I've been wanting to give this old house to somebody, and I'll give it to you.' "

My mother said, "Well, if what you're trying to tell me is you think your father and I should buy a house, that's ridiculous. Someday you'll have your own house, but it's too late for us."

So I said to Mary Smith, "Now there used to be an old house down here. An old man lived there all alone." And she said, "Well, that's the house right next door. He died. There's a Greek family there now and they've remodeled. That's probably why you didn't recognize it."

Of course I wanted to say right then, I'll take it. But we hadn't heard the price yet. So then we went downstairs and sat in the middle room under the chandelier that I now have in my dining room, and they couldn't keep their eyes off the baby—they passed him from one to the other—how beautiful he was, you know. These were three spinsters, they'd never married.

Anyway, they wanted eighteen thousand dollars for the house. And we left with high hopes, and the real estate agent said we'd need about six thousand for the down payment, but we only had fifteen hundred. So we went home and we talked about how wonderful it would be to get that house, instead of the little house in Hinsdale, which we could afford. This was a house we could stay in for our whole life.

Mary, the real estate lady, told her boss she knew she was going to sell the house to us. But her boss said, "I think you've got to find somebody else. I don't think they'll come up with the money." Of course you have to understand that six thousand dollars then was a lot more than it is today.

It got a little confusing sometimes. There was Mary Clark, Mary Smith, and Mary the real estate woman.

One day Mary Smith called. She said, "I called up your landlady and the things she said about you you would not say about your worst enemy. I know it's not true, I know she's just trying to make trouble for you. So I said to myself, we'll just reduce the asking price. Then I told my sisters and we've all agreed. We'll come down to fifteen thousand dollars." That way we would only need a five-thousand-dollar down payment. So the landlady did us a favor.

Vince went down to work the next day. And he went to lunch and he told all of his friends about the house. But he said, "I'm not sure I have enough for the down payment." One by one, they kept making offers, I'll lend you five hundred, or a thousand, two hundred, three hundred. And suddenly he had quite a bit of money that he could get. So he came home very happy.

That was in March.

The real estate office was on Madison near Waller. And I remember that on my fortieth birthday, May 12th, we put earnest money down on the house. So I said, "Life really does begin at forty." And I really believed it that day.

The day of the closing we went to Chicago Title and Trust downtown. Well, Vince had all these checks from his friends. He had more than he needed. But he had to get them certified. So he told me, "I'm going to be late. I'm going bank to bank. So when you get there tell them I had a case that I just couldn't get out of, and I'll be there as quickly as I can." It was his own personal case. My case. After all, he was getting a house for me, wasn't he?

Anyhow, so there were the three Smith sisters, our real estate agent, the head of the real estate firm, their lawyer, the Smiths' lawyer, and there was me. And they said, "Where is the buyer?" I said, "Well, he came downtown with me but he had a case that he just had to do. But he said to tell you he will be here as quickly as he can."

So they all sat around talking, and looking at the clock. And me, I'm a nervous wreck. The real estate man said, "We've often waited for the seller but we've never waited for the buyer." And I said, "Well, I'm here. I'm buying too."

So finally Vince comes. And we're in a partition with glass all the way around. He's got his hat in his hand, and he walks inside the room and he puts his hat on the hat rack and it fell to the ground. The rack was on the other side of the glass.

So that made everybody laugh and that cleared the air.

And that was it. It didn't take us too long to get through the closing.

Vince went to his office. And Mary, the real estate woman, asked if I would walk to Union Station with her. She said, "I'm getting a one-way ticket. I'm going to join the convent."

I said, "You are?"

She said, "Well, I have to tell you how it happened. I used you. I've been wanting to go for years and I decided if I could sell the house to the Clarks then I would consider that a sign that I should go to the convent."

So we walked through the Loop and in all the noise of downtown I could hear a song. "This is the day the Lord has made. Let us rejoice and be glad." That's why I have it on my refrigerator. It's an Easter song.

I never saw Mary after that. Years later, when we were selling the house, we invited the Smiths over, and they had kept in touch with her. She had gone to the convent but she'd only stayed for a few years. And they said that now she was married and had a couple of kids of her own.

Softly, As I Leave You

Pegge was in the convent. She went in with three or four of her friends. They were going to be Sisters of Mercy. They all left eventually. But Peg was the first to go.

I remember she was having trouble with some of the nuns. One day she was wearing tennis shoes or loafers and one of the nuns said, "What are you doing wearing those shoes?" And Peg said, "My others are at the shoemaker." And the sister said, "You mean to tell me you came to this convent with only one pair of dress shoes?" And Peg said, "I've never had more than one pair at a time in my life." And that was true in our house. There were too many to buy.

There were other things too, and eventually she decided to leave. This was in July of 1967. Vince talked to her and said, "Don't make a big decision like that unless you've thought it through. So think about it until the end of the week and if you still want to come home, we'll be very happy to have you."

So on Friday she called and she had decided she would leave. When we got there on Saturday she was standing outside the convent with her trunk alongside of her. Vince put it in the back of the station wagon. The three of us got into the car and Peg threw her arms around us and started to sing. And we sang all the way from Evergreen Park to the Loop without ever stopping.

It was when he put the trunk in the car that I noticed Vince was limping. After we got home, I asked him what was wrong. He said he didn't know but he had called the doctor and he would go see him on Monday.

He went to the doctor and he ended up in the hospital for three weeks. It had nothing to do with his leg. He had malignant hypertension. So for the next fourteen months, he was in and out of the hospital seven or eight times. He'd be home for a couple of weeks, then in for a couple of weeks. It was really providential that Peg was home. She took his blood pressure and called the doctor and told him what it was, and when he was in the hospital, she went every day.

We celebrated our twenty-fifth wedding anniversary. March 1968. We had a big party, with lots of friends. The West Side riots were in April. And we could see the West Side burning from his hospital room.

In June Kevin graduated from grade school and Maude and Michele, our foster daughter, graduated from college. Vince was back in the hospital. After the awards night at Loyola we all went to visit. Maude and Michele both got awards and Vince gave Maude a watch. She was happy but she was sort of holding back. Then he gave one to Michele too. And then Maude was ecstatic. She'd been afraid Michele wasn't getting anything.

In July we had the Ryan family picnic and he was out of the hospital and he came.

In August Vince's friends had a surprise party for his fiftieth birthday. They told him it was for Phil, whose birthday was a few days earlier, but when we walked in to Phil's office they started singing Happy Birthday and Vince realized that it was his party. All his friends were there.

He enjoyed the party. There was food and cake. It was very nice. But he got tired after a while and he went into one of the offices to lie down. They asked me what they could do for him. I said, "Tell him how you feel about him."

He was lying on a couch and they started going in one at a time—it looked like a line going to confession—and talking to him individually. When we got home Vince was very pleased. He said he'd heard things that he'd never heard about himself. So I guess they went all out.

I remember when we were leaving, he thanked Phil and Phil said, "Friends, Vince. Friends."

His birthday was a few days later, August 16th. And there was a party at the house. And then right after that he went back in the hospital and he was very bad. I suggested to the doctor that we take him to the Mayo Clinic. But two or three doctors talked to me and said it wouldn't do any good. They were well aware of what was wrong with him and there was nothing they could do for him at Mayo that they couldn't do in Chicago. And there was nothing else they could do for him. So we gave up on that idea. And we notified his relatives in California.

Aunt Agnes and Rosalyn came in from California. And I remember Maude and Michele, the whole crowd of them, Mary Jo, Kathleen, they're all jammed in the doorway between the dining room and the kitchen. And they're arguing about Mayor

Daley and the Democratic convention, which was going on at the time. Aunt Agnes says to Mary Jo, who was sixteen, "Young lady, you shouldn't be bothering your mind with this kind of stuff. You should be working on your catechism."

I can't remember what Mary Jo said but I know they said, "We always talk about politics with our father."

Lenore said, "He always made everyone feel seven feet tall." The expression is *ten feet tall*. But in the poem I was writing about him at the time I used *seven feet tall*. Lenore was his cousin. They grew up together. She was younger than Vince.

My son Vincent was in the navy, and I was taking a nap one day and he said something. I said, "Did Vincent come yet?" He said, "Vincent is here." I opened my eyes and there he was. So we went down to the hospital.

We put Vince in a wheelchair and took him to the windows, where we could see all the burned-out buildings from the riots.

Sam came—he used to work with Vince—and they started playing charades. He thought Vince was very up on it and wasn't so bad. But it was after that that I started staying all night. I wanted to be with him when the end came.

Every day as I sat beside his bed, I worked on my poem. It's the only one I ever really wrote. It's hanging on the wall in my bedroom.

> *I sit beside his bed and wonder where the*
> *thirty years have gone*
> *Living, loving and begetting*
> *I remember other days*
> *when we walked through the snow that hadn't been walked on*
> *or sat on a park bench with an umbrella overhead*
> *or had the first drink-of-the-spring at the park fountain.*
> *And studied and dreamed of things to come.*

> Came the war, he went away
> but not too far, and we enjoyed the Southern sun
> and shared our life, a daughter
> Seven more there are, who love him now, and asked
> to choose, he couldn't
> each seven feet tall, because of him, their father.

He sang. He was singing one of the songs that my mother used to sing to the kids. And then he sang "When the Saints Go Marching In." The doctor said it was nature letting him out easy.

They'd come around every day to take his blood. It wasn't going to help Vince any, not at that stage. One day I told one of them, "His blood isn't going to do you a bit of good." I went out to the desk and told the nurses to quit taking it. And when the doctor came in they told him and he said, "She's right. Quit."

I stayed for a week in the hospital, day and night. And Peg would come and stay while I went downstairs and slept on a couch. They had rooms down there with couches and a few chairs.

So I'd sleep a couple of hours and then I'd come upstairs. So on the seventeenth of September, I came up. Usually Peg would leave but that day Vince was more awake than usual even though we knew he wasn't really awake. He wasn't himself but he was better than he had been. We stood by the side of the bed for an hour or more, all holding hands. We were having a good time, laughing and talking. I remember he told Peg she was beautiful.

A nurse came in. She said she was just back from her vacation and she was going to give Vince a bath, a sponge bath in bed. And so the two of us decided to go down and have breakfast in the cafeteria.

I'd been eating whatever came up on the tray for a week so it was delightful to have a real breakfast. This was the only time we had breakfast together. We weren't anxious at all.

I said, "Let's not have coffee here. The coffee's better in the coffee shop." So we ate our breakfast and then we went to the coffee shop and when I went back for a second cup of coffee somehow or other I knocked a nurse's hat off. My sleeve caught it. I apologized and I gave the hat back and I realized it was the nurse that had been taking care of Vince upstairs. But she looked at me like she'd never seen me before.

I told Peg, "You know, the funniest thing just happened."

When we got off the elevator upstairs there were two doctors and three nurses waiting. "Mrs. Clark, I'm sorry to tell you, your husband passed away a few minutes ago."

So we went in and the room was all straightened up and they had him covered up and the bed straightened out. You knew he didn't die just that minute. We had been gone for quite a long time. We weren't thinking he was dying. That's why it was so easy to go to breakfast. He seemed so good. We weren't thinking he was going to go at any minute.

And then Dr. Coogan came in and told us how sorry he was. The cleaning lady was working in the hall and she came in, this little black cleaning lady. I used to talk to her every day. She'd say, "How is he doing today? How are you doing?"

I said, "I wanted so much to be with him."

She said, "You know why he died when you weren't here?" And I said, "No, I don't." She said, "He didn't want to hurt you."

I didn't tell the relatives that we weren't there. I figured they'd ask a million questions. Why weren't you there? We thought you'd be there? And I didn't have the answers.

Then a couple of weeks later I heard Frank Sinatra singing

Visiting Vince's Mother, Wedron, Illinois, 1939 or '40.

"Softly, As I Leave You." It's the story of a man leaving a woman. He says, "If I heard your voice, I couldn't go." And that solved my dilemma. I realized it was okay. That song and what the cleaning lady said. He waited till I was gone because he couldn't go while I was there.

Fortune-teller

In 1924 we moved around the corner to Sacramento Boulevard, to a bigger, nicer apartment, right on the corner of Lexington.

We had bay windows out on Sacramento. You could see both ways. It was great fun watching the fire wagons. Horses pulled them.

The middle window didn't open. The side windows did. So in order to wash the big middle window, my father got a plank and put it out a side window. He had my mother and us four kids sit on the end of the plank, and then he stood out on the other end of the plank and washed the window. Isn't that awful? He said that if any one of us got up that would be the end of him. Nobody budged. We were scared stiff while he was out there.

Once my mother went to a fortune-teller—the only time in her life—and afterwards she said, "Never, never, never go to a fortune-teller. It's the worst thing you can do." The fortune-teller told her that her husband would be hit by a car and probably killed. This was not long before Christmas. In our house the tree and everything were gotten after the kids went to bed on Christmas Eve, because Santa brought the tree along with the presents.

So after we went to sleep my father would go out and get the tree. They would decorate the tree, put the toys under it. Well, I'm sound asleep in bed. I'm ten years old. I still believe there's a Santa Claus. And my mother comes in and wakes me up and asks me if I will come to the window with her. So I walk in the front room and see the tree all decorated.

My father had gone across the boulevard to see how the tree looked. And Ma thought of the fortune-teller. What if a car hit him? What was she going to do? She was going to depend on me, a ten-year-old kid?

Anyway, he went out to see the tree, and he came back and said it looked fine. By then I was back in bed wondering.

I guess Ma was just petrified and she needed somebody to be with her—and she chose me. But that's how I found out there was no Santa Claus.

That was the same year Pa took Marge and me downtown to see the Christmas tree. This was before Christmas. The tree was on Michigan Avenue at Congress, where the Indians are. A great big, big Christmas tree. And afterwards he took us to a record shop, and he bought "That Old Gang of Mine" and "Last Night on the Back Porch."

You know that song?

> *I love her in the springtime*
> *And I love her in the fall*
> *But last night on the back porch*
> *I loved her best of all.*

And he used to play "That Old Gang of Mine."

Oh, how I'd love to see that old gang of mine
Oh, how I can't forget the times we sang "Sweet Adeline"
Good-bye forever, old sweethearts and pals.

*January 23, 1957, Vincent's tenth birthday. Maudemarie,
Vincent, Firpo (that's the dog), Pegge, Jack, Mary Jo, Kevin,
and Kathleen (in Mother's arms next to Father).*

RELATIONSHIPS TO MARY JO CLARK

Thomas McLaughlin—great-grandfather.
Mary—great-grandmother. She married Thomas McLaughlin in Ireland; died in Illinois in 1855.
Margaret Guilfoyle—Thomas McLaughlin's second wife. She had no children of her own but she helped raise his seven.

Philip Ryan—grandfather
Nancy McLaughlin—grandmother
Patrick Hennessy—grandfather
Catherine Houlihan—grandmother

Jack Ryan—father
Maud Hennessy—mother

Aunt Nell Hennessy—great-aunt, Patrick Hennessy's sister.
Aunt Nell Havern—great-aunt, Catherine Houlihan's sister.
Lillian, Eleanor, and **Marguerite** are her daughters. **Heggie** is Eleanor's husband.

Aunt Maggie—great-aunt, also Catherine Houlihan's sister. She married **Uncle Bill**.
Cousin Nora—Nora Houlihan, Maud Hennessy's first cousin. She married **Jim Kincaid**.

Thomas, Edward, James, Margaret, Anna, and **Rose Ryan**—aunts and uncles. These are the brothers and sisters of Jack Ryan. Anna (**Aunt Anna**) married Patrick McGovern (**Uncle Percy**).

Cousin Nancy and **Blanche, Phil, Will, Leo, Art, Jim,** and **Frank Ryan**—aunts and uncles; the children of Philip Ryan's brother **Patrick Ryan** and Nancy McLaughlin's sister, **Ellen McLaughlin**.

Margaret Mary (**Marge**) **Ryan**—oldest sister. She married Francis (**Bud**) **McIntyre**. They had one child, **Johnny**.

Rosemarie Ryan—youngest sister. She married **Thomas McLaughlin**. They had three children, **Tom, Pat,** and **Michael**.

Ed Ryan—younger brother. He married **Marguerite Kinney** (right, back cover photograph). They had three children, **Mary Jude, Marguerite (Peggy),** and **Jeanne**.

John, Loretta, and **James Ryan**—brothers and sisters who died within days of birth.

Vincent M. Clark—husband.

Margaret Gantes—Vince's mother. Her maiden name was McLaughlin.

Aunt Agnes and **Aunt May**—Vince's aunts. Margaret Gantes' sisters.

Lenore and **Rosalyn**—Vince's cousins. Aunt Agnes' daughters.

Maudemarie, Vincent, Margaret (Ryan/Pegge), John (Jack), Mary Jo (right, front cover photograph), **Kevin** (in arms, front cover photograph), and **Kathleen Clark**—children.

Michele Barale—foster daughter.

Catherine Conway—oldest friend. She married **Leo Higdon**. That's her in the middle on back cover of book. She lives in Florida today.